Collins

T0035750

Unlocking
MANDARIN CHINESE
with
Paul Noble

Published by Collins
An imprint of HarperCollins Publishers
Westerhill Road
Bishopbriggs
Glasgow G64 2QT

First edition 2020

10 9 8 7 6 5 4 3 2 1

© Paul Noble & Kai-Ti Noble 2020

ISBN 978-0-00-840816-9

Collins® is a registered trademark of
HarperCollins Publishers Limited

Typeset by Davidson Publishing Solutions,
Glasgow

Printed in Italy by Grafica Veneta S.p.A

A catalogue record for this book is available
from the British Library.

If you would like to comment on any aspect
of this book, please contact us at the given
address or online.
E-mail dictionaries@harpercollins.co.uk
www.facebook.com/collinsdictionary
@CollinsDict

Acknowledgements
Images from Shutterstock.

MANAGING EDITOR
Maree Airlie

CONTRIBUTORS
Joyce Littlejohn
Lin Luan

FOR THE PUBLISHER
Gerry Breslin
Kevin Robbins
Sheena Shanks

People who know no Chinese at all.

People who know some Chinese already.

People learning Chinese for the first time.

People coming back to the language after a break.

People who didn't like how languages were taught at school.

People who are amazed by just how closely grammar books resemble furniture assembly instructions.

Who is this book for?

People who think they can't learn a foreign language.

People who've listened to one of Paul Noble's audio courses.

People who haven't listened to one of Paul Noble's audio courses.

People who studied Chinese at school.

People who didn't study Chinese at school.

People curious about whether they can learn a language.

People who feel confused by the way languages are normally taught.

Contents

Did you know you
already speak Chinese?

Did you know you already speak Chinese?

Did you know you already speak Chinese? That you hear it in the street? That you've used it with your friends, with your family, at work, in the supermarket?

Were you aware of that fact?

Well, even if you weren't, it's nevertheless true.

Of course, you might not have realised at the time that what you were reading / saying / hearing was actually Chinese but I can prove to you that it was. Just take a look at these words below:

feng shui	chow mein	tofu	kung fu
typhoon	mahjong	lychee	dim sum
kowtow	ginseng	tai chi Zen	yin & yang

Have you read through them?
yes? Good.

Now, answer me this, are they:

A: English words
B: Chinese words
C: Both

Well, if you're reading this book then you're clearly already a highly intelligent person with good judgement, so you will have correctly chosen "C".

Yes, these are words that we have in English *but* they do of course originate from Chinese. And these are by no means isolated examples of words that are shared by both English and Chinese; rather they are merely the tip of a by no means tiny iceberg.

This is because not only are there many Chinese words that have come into English over the centuries, but there are also *even more* English words that have gone into Chinese.

So, if we begin by using these words, together with an extremely subtle method that shows you how to put them into sentences in a way that's almost effortless, then becoming competent at speaking Chinese becomes far, far easier.

The only thing that *you* will need to do to make this happen is to follow the three simple rules printed on the following pages. These rules will explain to you how to use this book so that you can begin unlocking the Chinese language for yourself in a matter of hours.

Well, what are you waiting for? Turn the page!

How to use this book — 3 Simple Rules

Using this book is extremely simple – and highly effective – *if* you follow its three simple rules.

If you don't want to follow them then I recommend that, instead of reading the book, you use it to prop up a wobbly coffee table, as it won't work if you don't follow the rules. Now get ready – because here's the first one!

Rule Number 1:

Don't skip anything!

Each and every little thing in this book has been put where it is, in a very particular order, for a very particular reason. So, if the book asks you to read or do something, then do it! Who's the teacher after all, you or me, eh? Also, each part of the book builds on and reinforces what came before it. So, if you start skipping sections, you will end up confused and lost! Instead, you should just take your time and gently work your way through the book at your own pace – *but without skipping anything!*

Step
by
Step

Rule Number 2:

Don't try to memorise anything!

Trying to jam things into your head is boring *and* it doesn't work. People often cram for tests and then forget everything the moment they walk out of the exam. Clearly, we don't want that happening here.

Instead, I have designed this book so that any word or idea taught in it will come up multiple times. So, you don't need to worry about trying to remember or memorise anything because the necessary repetition is actually already built-in. In fact, trying to memorise what you're learning is likely to hinder rather than help your progress.

So, just work your way through the book in a relaxed way and, if you happen to forget something, don't worry because, as I say, you will be reminded of it again, multiples times, later on.

Rule Number 3:
Cover up!

No, I'm not being a puritan grandmother and telling you to put on a long-sleeved cardigan. Instead, I'm asking you to take a bookmark or piece of paper and use it to cover up any **red text** that you come across as you work your way through the book.

These **red bits** are the answers to the various riddles, challenges, and questions that I will pose as I lead you into the Chinese language. If you read these answers without at least trying to work out the solutions to the various riddles and challenges first, then the book simply won't work for you!

So, make sure to use something to cover up the bits of **red text** in the book while you have a go at trying to work out the answers – it doesn't matter if you sometimes get them wrong because it is by trying to think out the answers that you will learn how to use the language.

Trust me on this, you will see that it works from the very first page!

Take a look at the page on the right to see how to use your bookmark or piece of paper to cover up correctly.

And, as I mentioned just a moment ago, "tofu" is:

豆腐
dòufu
(doe-foo)

So how would you say "You want tofu"?

你要豆腐。
Nǐ yào dòufu.
(nee yow doe-foo)

And again how would you say "You want chow mein"?

你要炒面。
Nǐ yào chǎo miàn.
(nee yow CHow mee-en)

"And" in Chinese is:

和
hé
(her)

Now again, what is "chow mein"?

炒面
chǎo miàn
(CHow mee-en)

And what is "tofu"?

豆腐
dòufu
(doe-foo)

And do you remember what "and" was?

和
hé
(her)

20

So how would you say "chow mein and tofu"?

炒面和豆腐
chǎo miàn hé dòufu
(CHow mee-en her doe-foo)

Now, once again, what is "you want"?

你要
nǐ yào
(nee yow)

So how would you say "You want chow mein and tofu"?

Make sure to cover up any red words, just like this!

你要
nǐ yào
(nee yow)

And what is "You want chow mein"?

你要炒面。
Nǐ yào chǎo miàn.
(nee yow CHow mee-en)

Now, as I said just a moment ago, if you want to turn this into a question and ask "Do you want chow mein?" all you need to do is to add a spoken question mark onto the end of this sentence. And that spoken question mark is the word "ma".

Let's use it now!

21

And, as I mentioned just a moment ago, "tofu" is:

豆腐
dòufu
(doe-foo)

So how would you say "You want tofu"?

你要豆腐。
Nǐ yào dòufu.
(nee yow doe-foo)

And again how would you say "You want chow mein"?

你要炒面。
Nǐ yào chǎo miàn.
(nee yow CHow mee-en)

"And" in Chinese is:

和
hé
(her)

Now again, what is "chow mein"?

炒面
chǎo miàn
(CHow mee-en)

And what is "tofu"?

豆腐
dòufu
(doe-foo)

And do you remember what "and" was?

和
hé
(her)

20

So how would you say "chow mein and tofu"?

炒面和豆腐
chǎo miàn hé dòufu
(CHow mee-en her doe-foo)

Now, once again, what is "you want"?

你要
nǐ yào
(nee yow)

So how would you say "You want chow mein and tofu"?

你要炒面和豆腐。
Nǐ yào chǎo miàn hé dòufu.
(nee yow CHow mee-en her doe-foo)

Then, having tried to work out the answer, uncover and check!

And what is "You want chow mein"?

你要炒面。
Nǐ yào chǎo miàn.
(nee yow CHow mee-en)

Now, as I said just a moment ago, if you want to turn this into a question and ask "Do you want chow mein?" all you need to do is to add a spoken question mark onto the end of this sentence. And that spoken question mark is the word "ma".

Let's use it now!

21

Oh, and just one more thing before we begin...

There's just one more thing I need to let you know before we begin and it's to do with how I've written the Chinese in this book.

Once you begin, you'll see that each English sentence in the book has three translations of it into Chinese. For example:

I want chow mein. 我要炒面。

Wǒ yào chǎo miàn.

(wor yow CHow mee-en)

Now you might be wondering, why are there three different versions? What are they for?

Well, to begin with, please be aware that all three versions say exactly the same thing in Chinese.

The top version is simply a translation of the English that has been written in simplified Chinese characters. This is the written form of Chinese used in Mainland China.

The middle version is a translation of the English that has been written in the official, Romanised form of Chinese, known as "Pinyin". It is used by non-Chinese people to read the language. It also includes tone marks to let you know which tone to use for each syllable (you'll learn about the tones later on).

The final, bottom version of the Chinese is my own personal pronunciation guide, which is designed to show you how to pronounce the language if you can't already read Chinese characters (a virtual certainty) and are unfamiliar with Pinyin (a distinct possibility). Basically, it's the Chinese words written in English letters according to how they would probably be spelled if they were English words. So, a bit of extra pronunciation help, in case you need it.

Anyway, these are the three versions of Chinese you'll see throughout the book – please use whichever one helps you most!

Okay now, let's begin!

CHAPTER 1

Do you want a bit of fried rice?

> **Do you want a bit of fried rice?**
> **I dunno. Maybe...**

The two English sentences above aren't that complicated, are they?
Or are they...?

Well, I have taught many people over the years, ranging from those who know no Chinese at all through to those who may have spent several years trying to learn the language. And yet, whether they have studied the language before or not, more or less none of them arrive in my classroom able to construct seemingly simple sentences, such as the two above, when I first meet them.

Admittedly, they might know how to say other far less useful things, like "I'm 37 years old and have two sisters" – an unusual conversation opener for an adult from my perspective – but they nevertheless can't ask someone if they want a bit of fried rice or give a non-committal response in reply.

Well, in just a few minutes' time, you will be able to do this – even if you've never learned any Chinese before.

Just remember though: ***don't* skip anything, *don't* waste your time trying to memorise anything but *do* use your bookmark to cover up anything red you find on each page.**

Okay now, let's begin!

"You want" in Chinese is:

你要
nǐ yào
(pronounced "nee yow"[1])

---

1   Under each set of Chinese words, you'll find pronunciation guidance in brackets. If there's something that's particularly tricky to pronounce, however, I'll also add a little footnote like this one to give you some extra help. I'm going to do this now in fact, to help you with the "**ow**" at the end of "**nee yow**". Whenever I write an "**ow**" in the pronunciation guidance, you should pronounce that "**ow**" like the "**ow**" in the English word "**now**". You'll see that in the Pinyin this sort of sound is spelled "ao" and, if that works for you then fine but, if not, my pronunciation guide underneath should hopefully make the correct pronunciation of the word even clearer!

And "chow mein" in Mandarin Chinese is:

炒面
chǎo miàn
(pronounced "CHow mee-en")

So, knowing this, how would you say, "You want chow mein"?

你要炒面。
Nǐ yào chǎo miàn.
(nee yow CHow mee-en)

Did you remember to cover up the red words while you worked out the answer?

"Tofu" in Chinese is:

豆腐
dòufu
(doe-foo)

Now again, what was "you want"?

你要
nǐ yào
(nee yow)

And, as I mentioned just a moment ago,
"tofu" is:

豆腐
dòufu
(*doe-foo*)

So how would you say "You want tofu"?

你要豆腐。
Nǐ yào dòufu.
(*nee yow doe-foo*)

And again how would you say "You want chow mein"?

你要炒面。
Nǐ yào chǎo miàn.
(*nee yow CHow mee-en*)

"And" in Chinese is:

和
hé
(*her*)

Now again, what is "chow mein"?

炒面
chǎo miàn
(*CHow mee-en*)

And what is "tofu"?

豆腐
dòufu
(*doe-foo*)

And do you remember what "and" was?

和
hé
(*her*)

So how would say "chow mein and tofu"?

炒面和豆腐
chǎo miàn hé dòufu
(CHow mee-en her doe-foo)

Now, once again, what is "you want"?

你要
nǐ yào
(nee yow)

So how would you say "You want chow mein and tofu"?

你要炒面和豆腐。
Nǐ yào chǎo miàn hé dòufu.
(nee yow CHow mee-en her doe-foo)

If you want to ask a question in Chinese, it's extremely easy because all you need to do is to add a spoken question mark onto the end of the sentence. I'll show you what I mean.

First of all, remind me, what is "you want"?

你要
nǐ yào
(nee yow)

And what is "You want chow mein"?

你要炒面。
Nǐ yào chǎo miàn.
(nee yow CHow mee-en)

Now, as I said just a moment ago, if you want to turn this into a question and ask "Do you want chow mein?" all you need to do is to add a spoken question **ma**rk onto the end of this sentence. And that spoken question **ma**rk is the word "ma".

Let's use it now!

First of all, again how would you say "You want chow mein"?

你要炒面。
Nǐ yào chǎo miàn.
(nee yow CHow mee-en)

Now add "ma" onto the end of this sentence and by doing so ask "Do you want chow mein?" – literally you'll say "You want chow mein ma?" Do that now!

你要炒面吗？
Nǐ yào chǎo miàn ma?
(nee yow CHow mee-en mah[2])

What is "tofu"?

豆腐
dòufu
(doe-foo)

So how would you say "Do you want tofu?" – literally "You want tofu ma?"

你要豆腐吗？
Nǐ yào dòufu ma?
(nee yow doe-foo mah)

Do you remember how to say "and" in Chinese?

和
hé
(her)

So how would you say "chow mein *and* tofu"?

炒面和豆腐
chǎo miàn hé dòufu
(CHow mee-en her doe-foo)

---

2   Whenever you see a word in the pronunciation guidance ending with "ah" – such as with the spoken
    question mark here (spelled by me as "mah") – you should always pronounce that word so that it rhymes
    with the English word "ah", as in "Ah, I understand." So, "ma" should sound like the "ma" in "mark" not like the
    "ma" in "mat!"

And how would you say "You want chow mein and tofu"?

你要炒面和豆腐。

Nǐ yào chǎo miàn hé dòufu.

(nee yow CHow mee-en her doe-foo)

And now once again turn this into a question by adding "ma" onto the end of it and ask "Do you want chow mein and tofu?" – literally "You want chow mein and tofu ma?"

你要炒面和豆腐吗？

Nǐ yào chǎo miàn hé dòufu ma?

(nee yow CHow mee-en her doe-foo mah)

Excellent!

So, we've now talked quite a bit about chow mein but have you actually ever eaten it? If not, you'll find it's useful to know that "chow mein" are actually fried noodles, and that is what "chow mein" literally means: "fried noodles".

Knowing this fact is very useful to us because it gives us the words both for "fried" and "noodles" in Chinese. So, if "chow mein" – "**chǎo miàn**" – literally means "fried noodles" then what is the Chinese word for "fried"?

炒

chǎo

(CHow[3])

"Rice" in Chinese is:

饭

fàn

(fan)

So how do you think you'd say "fried rice"?

炒饭

chǎo fàn

(CHow fan)

---

3 By the way, you'll perhaps have noticed how, in the pronunciation guidance, I've spelled CHow with a capital CH. I've done this to help you improve your pronunciation still further. Whenever you see a "CH" written in capitals in the pronunciation guide, this means that you should make a "ch" sound just as you would in English except that, when you do it, you will touch your tongue to the roof of the mouth. The resulting sound may seem a little unfamiliar, a slightly weird kind of "ch", but that is the sound you're aiming for. So, whenever you see a capital CH, don't simply make an ordinary English "ch" sound but from now on instead say "ch" while touching your tongue to the roof of your mouth.

And how would you say "You want fried rice"?

你要炒饭。
Nǐ yào chǎo fàn.
(nee yow CHow fan)

How about "Do you want fried rice?" – literally "You want fried rice ma?"

你要炒饭吗？
Nǐ yào chǎo fàn ma?
(nee yow CHow fan mah)

"Do you want fried rice and tofu?"

你要炒饭和豆腐吗？
Nǐ yào chǎo fàn hé dòufu ma?
(nee yow CHow fan her doe-foo mah)

And once again, just on its own, what is "you want" in Chinese?

你要
nǐ yào
(nee yow)

So, if "**nǐ yào**" means "you want", then what is the Chinese word for "want"?

要
yào
(yow)

The word for "I" in Chinese is:

我
wǒ
(wor)

So how would you say "I want"?

我要
wǒ yào
(wor yow)

How about "I want fried rice"?

我要炒饭。
Wǒ yào chǎo fàn.
(wor yow CHow fan)

Again, what is "and"?

和
hé
(her)

So how would you say "I want fried rice and tofu"?

我要炒饭和豆腐。
Wǒ yào chǎo fàn hé dòufu.
(wor yow CHow fan her doe-foo)

"Not" in Chinese is:

不
bù
(boo)

Now again, what is "I want"?

我要
wǒ yào
(wor yow)

And what was "not"?

不
bù
(boo)

If you want to say "I don't want" in Chinese, you'll literally say "I not want".
How do you think you would say that?

我不要
wǒ bù yào
(wor boo yow)

And how would you say "I don't want fried rice" – literally "I not want fried rice"?

我不要炒饭。
Wǒ bù yào chǎo fàn.
(wor boo yow CHow fan)

How about "I don't want fried noodles"?

我不要炒面。
Wǒ bù yào chǎo miàn.
(wor boo yow CHow mee-en)

And "I don't want fried noodles and tofu"?

我不要炒面和豆腐。
Wǒ bù yào chǎo miàn hé dòufu.
(wor boo yow CHow mee-en her doe-foo)

What is "you want"?

你要
nǐ yào
(nee yow)

And again what is "not"?

不
bù
(boo)

So how do you think you'd say "you don't want" (literally "you not want")?

你不要
nǐ bù yào
(nee boo yow)

How about "You don't want fried rice"?

你不要炒饭。
Nǐ bù yào chǎo fàn.
(nee boo yow CHow fan)

And "You don't want tofu"?

你不要豆腐。
Nǐ bù yào dòufu.
(nee boo yow doe-foo)

What is the spoken question **ma**rk in Chinese?

吗
ma
(mah)

And again, what is "you don't want", literally "you not want"?

你不要
nǐ bù yào
(nee boo yow)

And how would you say, "You don't want fried rice"?

你不要炒饭。
Nǐ bù yào chǎo fàn.
(nee boo yow CHow fan)

Turn this sentence into a question now by adding "ma" onto the end of it and ask "Don't you want fried rice?" – literally "You not want fried rice ma?"

你不要炒饭吗？
Nǐ bù yào chǎo fàn ma?
(nee boo yow CHow fan mah)

And how would you say "Don't you want fried noodles?"

你不要炒面吗？
Nǐ bù yào chǎo miàn ma?
(nee boo yow CHow mee-en mah)

What about "Don't you want fried noodles and tofu?"

你不要炒面和豆腐吗？
Nǐ bù yào chǎo miàn hé dòufu ma?
(nee boo yow CHow mee-en her doe-foo mah)

And going back a step, what is simply "you want"?

你要
nǐ yào
(nee yow)

And so if "**nǐ yào**" is "you want" then what is "you" in Chinese?

你
nǐ
(nee)

"Know" in Chinese is:

知道
zhīdào
(ZHi-dow[4])

So how would you say "you know"?

你知道
nǐ zhīdào
(nee ZHi-dow)

What is "I"?

我
wǒ
(wor)

So how would you say "I know"?

我知道。
Wǒ zhīdào.
(wor ZHi-dow)

---

4   Whenever you see a "ZH" written in the pronunciation guide in this book, you should pronounce it more or less like the "j" in "jerk" except that while you make that "j" sound, you should also touch your tongue to the roof of your mouth. The sound you make will probably seem slightly weird - *that's* the "ZH" sound! (And by the way, whenever you come across any capitalised letters in the pronunciation guidance, this means that those are letters that you should pronounce with your tongue touched to the roof of your mouth. So far, we've encountered SH and ZH. Later on in the book, there will be just one more.)

What is "you want"?

你要
nǐ yào
(nee yow)

And so how would you say "You want fried rice"?

你要炒饭。
 Nǐ yào chǎo fàn.
(nee yow CHow fan)

And again, what was "I know"?

我知道。
Wǒ zhīdào.
(wor ZHi-dow)

So how would you say "I know you want fried rice"?

我知道你要炒饭。
Wǒ zhīdào nǐ yào chǎo fàn.
(wor ZHi-dow nee yow CHow fan)

How about "I know you want fried noodles"?

我知道你要炒面。
Wǒ zhīdào nǐ yào chǎo miàn.
(wor ZHi-dow nee yow CHow mee-en)

And now again, just on its own, what is "I want"?

我要
wǒ yào
(wor yow)

And what is "not"?

不
bù
(boo)

And so how would you say "I don't want"?

我不要
wǒ bù yào
(wor boo yow)

And again what is "I know"?

我知道。
Wǒ zhīdào.
(wor ZHi-dow)

So how do you think you would say "I don't know" – literally "I not know"?

我不知道。
Wǒ bù zhīdào.
(wor boo ZHi-dow)

How about "You don't know"?

你不知道。
Nǐ bù zhīdào.
(nee boo ZHi-dow)

Turn that into a question by adding "ma" onto the end of it and ask "Don't you know?"

你不知道吗？
Nǐ bù zhīdào ma?
(nee boo ZHi-dow mah)

And now answer that question, saying "I don't know".

我不知道。
Wǒ bù zhīdào.
(wor boo ZHi-dow)

Now once again, how would you say "You want fried rice"?

你要炒饭。
Nǐ yào chǎo fàn.
(nee yow CHow fan)

And "Do you want fried rice?"

你要炒饭吗？
Nǐ yào chǎo fàn ma?
(*nee yow* CHow *fan mah*)

"A little" or "a bit of" in Chinese is:

一点
yīdiǎn
(*ee-dee-en*)

Now again, what is "fried rice"?

炒饭
chǎo fàn
(CHow *fan*)

And, as I said, "a little" or "a bit of" is:

一点
yīdiǎn
(*ee-dee-en*)

So how would you say "a bit of fried rice"?

一点炒饭
yīdiǎn chǎo fàn
(*ee-dee-en* CHow *fan*)

And so how would you say "Do you want a bit of fried rice?"

你要一点炒饭吗？
Nǐ yào yīdiǎn chǎo fàn ma?
(*nee yow ee-dee-en* CHow *fan mah*)

And how about "Do you want a bit of tofu?" / "Do you want a little tofu?"

你要一点豆腐吗？
Nǐ yào yīdiǎn dòufu ma?
(*nee yow ee-dee-en doe-foo mah*)

And "Do you want a bit of chow mein?" / "Do you want a little chow mein?"

你要一点炒面吗?

Nǐ yào yīdiǎn chǎo miàn ma?

(nee yow ee-dee-en CHow mee-en mah)

How would you answer this question saying "I don't know"?

我不知道。

Wǒ bù zhīdào.

(wor boo ZHi-dow)

"Maybe" in Chinese is:

也许

yěxǔ

(ye-shü[5])

So how would you say "I don't know. Maybe."?

我不知道。也许。

Wǒ bù zhīdào. Yěxǔ.

(wor boo ZHi-dow. ye-shü)

And again, what is "a little" or "a bit of"?

一点

yīdiǎn

(ee-dee-en)

And "a bit of fried rice"?

一点炒饭

yīdiǎn chǎo fàn

(ee-dee-en CHow fan)

---

5   Whenever you see a "ü" in the pronunciation guidance, it means that you need to round your lips, as though you're about to whistle, but, instead of whistling say "ee" *but keep your lips rounded while you say it*. The weird sound that you get is the "ü" sound. So, to say "shü", round your lips and say "shee" **while keeping your lips rounded**. As I say, it will sound weird!

And so how would you say "Do you want a bit of fried rice?"

你要一点炒饭吗？
Nǐ yào yīdiǎn chǎo fàn ma?
(*nee yow ee-dee-en* CHow *fan mah*)

Do you remember what "maybe" was?

也许
yěxǔ
(*ye-shü*)

So how would you say "I don't know. Maybe."?

我不知道。也许。
Wǒ bù zhīdào. Yěxǔ.
(*wor boo* ZHi-*dow. ye-shü*)

Now, let's put all this together and return to that little exchange from the beginning of the chapter.

How would someone ask you "Do you want a bit of fried rice?"

你要一点炒饭吗？
Nǐ yào yīdiǎn chǎo fàn ma?
(*nee yow ee-dee-en* CHow *fan mah*)

Answer them, saying "I don't know. Maybe."

我不知道。也许。
Wǒ bù zhīdào. Yěxǔ.
(*wor boo* ZHi-*dow. ye-shü*)

So, there you go – you can now construct the sentences that we started the chapter with – and, as you will soon discover, this is only the very beginning of your journey into Chinese!

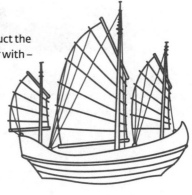

You just learned how to say (amongst other things) "Do you want a bit of fried rice?" Having done this, we are now going to move on to expand what you can say through the use of additional "building blocks".

The new building blocks you are going to learn will allow you to begin instantly expanding your range of expression in the Chinese language.

So far, some of the building blocks you have already learned include:

And you already know how to use these building blocks to construct a sentence. So, once again, how would you say "Do you want a bit of fried rice?"

So, you already know how to build the four building blocks above into a sentence. Take a look now at the six new building blocks below. Just have a glance over them and then I'll show you how we're going to add these into the mix of what we've learned so far.

他要
tā yào
(tah yow)
he wants

茶
chá
(CHah)
tea

她要
tā yào
(tah yow)
she wants

可乐
kělè
(ker-ler)
cola / coke[6]

咖啡
kāfēi
(kah-fay)
coffee

多一点
duō yīdiǎn
(dwor ee-dee-en)
a bit more / a little more[7]

Okay, first things first: please don't to try to memorise them. No, no, no! Instead, I simply want you to play with your building blocks. After all, that's what building blocks are for, isn't it?

And the way you're going to play with them is like this: on the next page they have been put into four piles and all I want you to do is to make sentences with them. **You'll do this by each time using one building block from the first pile, one from the second, one from the third, and one from the fourth**.

You will find that you can say a lot of different things using them in this way and it's up to you what sentences you make. The only thing I want you to make sure you do is to use every building block at least once and, also, please don't bother writing down the sentences you make. Instead, say them out loud, or, if you're not in a place where you can do this, say them in your head. Now, off you go; make as many sentences as you can!

---

6   I have written "cola / coke" in the pronunciation guidance as being pronounced "ker-ler". To get the pronunciation right, pronounce the "ker" part like the "ker" at the end of the English word "baker", and the "ler" part like the "ler" at the end of the English word "ruler".

7   Literally "more a bit" / "more a little".

1

你要
Nǐ yào
(nee yow)
You want

她要
Tā yào
(tah yow)
She wants

他要
Tā yào
(tah yow)
He wants

2

一点
yīdiǎn
(ee-dee-en)
a little / a bit of

多一点
duō yīdiǎn
(dwor ee-dee-en)
a bit more /
a little more

3

咖啡
kāfēi
(kah-fay)
coffee

茶
chá
(CHah)
tea

可乐
kělè
(ker-ler)
cola / coke

4

吗?
ma?
(mah)
spoken
question mark

The Checklist

You have now reached the final part of Chapter 1. Once you have finished this short section you will not only have completed your first chapter but you will also understand how this book works as the other chapters follow the same pattern, with your Chinese getting ever more sophisticated as you complete each chapter.

The section you are now on will be the final part of each chapter and is what I call "The Checklist". It involves nothing more than a read-through of a selection of some of the words or expressions you have so far encountered.

You will actually see the checklist twice. The first time you will see that the Chinese words are written in **black** (on the left-hand side) and that the English words are written in red (on the right-hand side) – and you know what red means! Cover up!

So, what I want you to do here is to cover up the English words (which are written in red on the right-hand side) while you read through the list of Chinese words on the left. Read through them all, from the top of the list to the bottom, and see if you can recall what they mean in English (uncover one red word at a time to check if you've remembered the meaning correctly). If you can go through the entire list, giving the correct English meaning for each of the Chinese words / expressions **without making more than 3 mistakes in total**, then you're done. If not, then go through the list again. Keep doing this, either working from the top of the list to bottom or from the bottom to the top (it doesn't matter which) until you can do it **without making more than 3 mistakes**.

Got it? Then let's go!

你 **nǐ** (nee)	you
要 **yào** (yow)	want
你要 **Nǐ yào** (nee yow)	You want
炒 **chǎo** (CHow)	fried
面 **miàn** (mee-en)	noodles
炒面 **chǎo miàn** (CHow mee-en)	fried noodles / chow mein
你要炒面。 **Nǐ yào chǎo miàn.** (nee yow CHow mee-en)	You want fried noodles / chow mein.
豆腐 **dòufu** (doe-foo)	tofu
你要豆腐。 **Nǐ yào dòufu.** (nee yow doe-foo)	You want tofu.

吗？ **ma?** (mah)	spoken question mark
你要豆腐吗？ **Nǐ yào dòufu ma?** (nee yow doe-foo mah)	Do you want tofu?
和 **hé** (her)	and
你要炒面和豆腐吗？ **Nǐ yào chǎo miàn hé dòufu ma?** (nee yow CHow mee-en her doe-foo mah)	Do you want fried noodles and tofu?
饭 **fàn** (fan)	rice
炒饭 **chǎo fàn** (CHow fan)	fried rice
你要炒饭和豆腐吗？ **Nǐ yào chǎo fàn hé dòufu ma?** (nee yow CHow fan her doe-foo mah)	Do you want fried rice and tofu?
不 **bù** (boo)	not
你不要炒饭和豆腐吗？ **Nǐ bù yào chǎo fàn hé dòufu ma?** (nee boo yow CHow fan her doe-foo mah)	Don't you want fried rice and tofu?
我 **wǒ** (wor)	I
我要 **Wǒ yào** (wor yow)	I want
我要炒饭和豆腐。 **Wǒ yào chǎo fàn hé dòufu.** (wor yow CHow fan her doe-foo)	I want fried rice and tofu.

我不要 **Wǒ bù yào** (wor *boo* yow)	I *don't* want
我不要炒饭和豆腐。 **Wǒ bù yào chǎo fàn hé dòufu.** (wor *boo* yow CHow fan her *doe-foo*)	I *don't* want fried rice and tofu.
我知道。 **Wǒ zhīdào.** (wor ZHi-dow)	I know.
我知道你要炒面。 **Wǒ zhīdào nǐ yào chǎo miàn.** (wor ZHi-dow nee yow CHow mee-en)	I know you want fried noodles.
我不知道。 **Wǒ bù zhīdào.** (wor *boo* ZHi-dow)	I *don't* know.
也许 **yěxǔ** (ye-shü)	maybe
我不知道。也许。 **Wǒ bù zhīdào. Yěxǔ.** (wor *boo* ZHi-dow. ye-shü)	I *don't* know. Maybe.
一点 **yīdiǎn** (ee-dee-en)	a little / a bit of
咖啡 **kāfēi** (kah-fay)	coffee
她要 **Tā yào** (tah yow)	She wants
她要一点咖啡。 **Tā yào yīdiǎn kāfēi.** (tah yow *ee-dee-en* kah-fay)	She wants a little coffee.
她要一点咖啡吗？ **Tā yào yīdiǎn kāfēi ma?** (tah yow *ee-dee-en* kah-fay mah)	Does she want a little coffee?

他要 **Tā yào** (tah yow)	He wants
茶 **chá** (CHah)	tea
他要一点茶。 **Tā yào yīdiǎn chá.** (tah yow ee-dee-en CHah)	He wants a little tea.
他要一点茶吗？ **Tā yào yīdiǎn chá ma?** (tah yow ee-dee-en CHah mah)	Does he want a little tea?
他要一点炒饭吗？ **Tā yào yīdiǎn chǎo fàn ma?** (tah yow ee-dee-en CHow fan mah)	Does he want a bit of fried rice?
多一点 **duō yīdiǎn** (dwor ee-dee-en)	a bit more / a little more
他要多一点炒饭吗？ **Tā yào duō yīdiǎn chǎo fàn ma?** (tah yow dwor ee-dee-en CHow fan mah)	Does he want a bit more fried rice?
可乐 **kělè** (ker-ler)	cola / coke
他要多一点可乐吗？ **Tā yào duō yīdiǎn kělè ma?** (tah yow dwor ee-dee-en ker-ler mah)	Does he want a little more coke?

Finished working through that checklist and made fewer than 3 mistakes? Yes? Wonderful!

As that's the case, what I now want you to do now is to repeat exactly the same process again below, except that this time you'll be reading through the *English* and trying to recall the Chinese. So, it will be the other way around. So, just relax and work your way up and down the list until you can give the correct Chinese translation for each of the *English* words / expressions **again without making more than 3 mistakes in total**. It's not a competition – and I'm not asking you to memorise them. No! Just look at the English words (on the left-hand side) while you cover up the red Chinese words on the right-hand side and see if you can remember how to say them in Chinese. You'll be surprised by how much you get right, even on the first try!

Okay, off you go!

you	你 **nǐ** (nee)
want	要 **yào** (yow)
You want	你要 **Nǐ yào** (nee yow)
fried	炒 **chǎo** (CHow)
noodles	面 **miàn** (mee-en)
fried noodles / chow mein	炒面 **chǎo miàn** (CHow mee-en)
You want fried noodles / chow mein.	你要炒面。 **Nǐ yào chǎo miàn.** (nee yow CHow mee-en)
tofu	豆腐 **dòufu** (doe-foo)
You want tofu.	你要豆腐。 **Nǐ yào dòufu.** (nee yow doe-foo)
spoken question mark	吗？ **ma?** (mah)

Do you want tofu?	你要豆腐吗？ **Nǐ yào dòufu ma?** (nee yow *doe-foo* mah)
and	和 **hé** (her)
Do you want fried noodles and tofu?	你要炒面和豆腐吗？ **Nǐ yào chǎo miàn hé dòufu ma?** (nee yow CHow mee-en her *doe-foo* mah)
rice	饭 **fàn** (fan)
fried rice	炒饭 **chǎo fàn** (CHow fan)
Do you want fried rice and tofu?	你要炒饭和豆腐吗？ **Nǐ yào chǎo fàn hé dòufu ma?** (nee yow CHow fan her *doe-foo* mah)
not	不 **bù** (boo)
Don't you want fried rice and tofu?	你不要炒饭和豆腐吗？ **Nǐ bù yào chǎo fàn hé dòufu ma?** (nee boo yow CHow fan her *doe-foo* mah)
I	我 **wǒ** (wor)
I want	我要 **Wǒ yào** (wor yow)
I want fried rice and tofu.	我要炒饭和豆腐。 **Wǒ yào chǎo fàn hé dòufu.** (wor yow CHow fan her *doe-foo*)

I don't want	我不要 **Wǒ bù yào** (wor boo yow)
I don't want fried rice and tofu.	我不要炒饭和豆腐。 **Wǒ bù yào chǎo fàn hé dòufu.** (wor boo yow CHow fan her doe-foo)
I know.	我知道。 **Wǒ zhīdào.** (wor ZHi-dow)
I know you want fried noodles.	我知道你要炒面。 **Wǒ zhīdào nǐ yào chǎo miàn.** (wor ZHi-dow nee yow CHow mee-en)
I don't know.	我不知道。 **Wǒ bù zhīdào.** (wor boo ZHi-dow)
maybe	也许 **yěxǔ** (ye-shü)
I don't know. Maybe.	我不知道。也许。 **Wǒ bù zhīdào. Yěxǔ.** (wor boo ZHi-dow. ye-shü)
a little / a bit of	一点 **yīdiǎn** (ee-dee-en)
coffee	咖啡 **kāfēi** (kah-fay)
She wants	她要 **Tā yào** (tah yow)
She wants a little coffee.	她要一点咖啡。 **Tā yào yīdiǎn kāfēi.** (tah yow ee-dee-en kah-fay)
Does she want a little coffee?	她要一点咖啡吗？ **Tā yào yīdiǎn kāfēi ma?** (tah yow ee-dee-en kah-fay mah)

He wants	他要 **Tā yào** (tah yow)
tea	茶 **chá** (CHah)
He wants a little tea.	他要一点茶。 **Tā yào yīdiǎn chá.** (tah yow ee-dee-en CHah)
Does he want a little tea?	他要一点茶吗？ **Tā yào yīdiǎn chá ma?** (tah yow ee-dee-en CHah mah)
Does he want a bit of fried rice?	他要一点炒饭吗？ **Tā yào yīdiǎn chǎo fàn ma?** (tah yow ee-dee-en CHow fan mah)
a bit more / a little more	多一点 **duō yīdiǎn** (dwor ee-dee-en)
Does he want a bit more fried rice?	他要多一点炒饭吗？ **Tā yào duō yīdiǎn chǎo fàn ma?** (tah yow dwor ee-dee-en CHow fan mah)
cola / coke	可乐 **kělè** (ker-ler)
Does he want a little more coke?	他要多一点可乐吗？ **Tā yào duō yīdiǎn kělè ma?** (tah yow dwor ee-dee-en ker-ler mah)

Well, that's it, you're done with Chapter 1! Now, don't try to hold onto or remember anything you've learned here. Everything you learn in earlier chapters will be brought up again and reinforced in later chapters. You don't need to do anything extra or make any effort to memorise anything. The book has been organised so that it does that for you. Now, off you go now and have a rest. You've earned it!

Between chapters, I'm going to be giving you various tips on language learning. These will range from useful tips about the Chinese language itself to advice on how to fit learning a language in with your daily routine. Ready for the first one? Here it is!

Tip Number One – Study (at least a little) every day!

Learning a language is like building a fire – if you don't tend to it, it will go out! So, once you have decided to learn a foreign language, you really should study it every day.

It doesn't have to be for a long time though. Just five or ten minutes each day will be enough, so long as you keep it up. Doing these five or ten minutes will stop you forgetting what you've already learned and, over time, will let you put more meat on the bones of what you're learning.

As for what counts towards those five or ten minutes, well that's up to you. Whilst you're working with this book, I would recommend that your five or ten minutes should be spent here, learning with me. Once you're done here, however, your five or ten minutes could be spent using an audio course, watching a Chinese video online, chatting with a Chinese-speaking acquaintance or attending a class if you want to learn in a more formal setting. The important thing though is to make sure that you do a little every day!

CHAPTER 2

He ordered tea, coffee, and dim sum but he didn't pay!

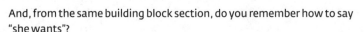

He ordered tea, coffee, and dim sum but he didn't pay!

The first chapter has shown you that you can learn how to build full and meaningful sentences in Chinese with relative ease. It also showed you how some Chinese words are already familiar to English speakers and you'll meet more of them here...

Now, please remind me, what is "I want"?

我要
wǒ yào
(wor yow)

And do you remember, from the building block section, what "coffee" is in Chinese?

咖啡
kāfēi
(kah-fay)

So how would you say "I want coffee"?

我要咖啡。
Wǒ yào kāfēi.
(wor yow kah-fay)

And, from the same building block section, do you remember how to say "she wants"?

她要
tā yào
(tah yow)

And so how would you say "She wants coffee"?

她要咖啡。
Tā yào kāfēi.
(tah yow kah-fay)

What is "a bit of" or "a little"?

一点
yīdiǎn
(*ee-dee-en*)

So what would be "She wants a little coffee"?

她要一点咖啡。
Tā yào yīdiǎn kāfēi.
(*tah yow ee-dee-en* kah-fay)

And how would you say "Does she want a little coffee?" – literally "She wants a little coffee ma?"

她要一点咖啡吗?
Tā yào yīdiǎn kāfēi ma?
(*tah yow ee-dee-en* kah-fay mah)

What is "a little more" / "a bit more"?

多一点
duō yīdiǎn
(*dwor ee-dee-en*)

So what would be "Does she want a little more coffee?"

她要多一点咖啡吗?
Tā yào duō yīdiǎn kāfēi ma?
(*tah yow dwor ee-dee-en* kah-fay mah)

What is "he wants"?

他要
tā yào
(*tah yow*)

And so how would you say "Does he want a little more coffee?"

他要多一点咖啡吗?
Tā yào duō yīdiǎn kāfēi ma?
(*tah yow dwor ee-dee-en* kah-fay mah)

What is "tea"?

茶
chá
(CHah)

And so what would be "Does he want tea?"

他要茶吗？
Tā yào chá ma?
(tah yow CHah mah)

Do you remember how to say "I know"?

我知道。
Wǒ zhīdào.
(wor ZHi-dow)

So how would you say "I know he wants tea"?

我知道他要茶。
Wǒ zhīdào tā yào chá.
(wor ZHi-dow tah yow CHah)

And how would you say "I know she wants tea"?

我知道她要茶。
Wǒ zhīdào tā yào chá.
(wor ZHi-dow tah yow CHah)

What is "cola" / "coke"?

可乐
kělè
(ker-ler)

So what would be "I know she wants coke"?

我知道她要可乐。
Wǒ zhīdào tā yào kělè.
(wor ZHi-dow tah yow ker-ler)

What is "I don't know"?

我不知道。
Wǒ bù zhīdào.
(wor boo ZHi-dow)

And what is "maybe"?

也许
yěxǔ
(ye-shü)

So how would you say "I don't know. Maybe."?

我不知道。也许。
Wǒ bù zhīdào. yěxǔ.
(wor boo ZHi-dow. ye-shü)

"Snack" or "a snack" in Chinese is:

点心
diǎnxīn
(dee-en-syin)

So how would you say "I want a snack"?

我要点心。
Wǒ yào diǎnxīn.
(wor yow dee-en-syin)

How about "You want a snack"?

你要点心。
Nǐ yào diǎnxīn.
(nee yow dee-en-syin)

And "Do you want a snack?"

你要点心吗?
Nǐ yào diǎnxīn ma?
(nee yow dee-en-syin mah)

How would you answer that question, saying "I don't know. Maybe."?

我不知道。也许。
Wǒ bù zhīdào. yěxǔ.
(wor boo ZHi-dow. ye-shü)

What is "I want"?

我要
wǒ yào
(wor yow)

And "I don't want"?

我不要
wǒ bù yào
(wor boo yow)

How about "I don't want a snack"?

我不要点心。
Wǒ bù yào diǎnxīn.
(wor boo yow dee-en-syin)

The wonderful world of dim sum...

Now, if you're lucky you will at some point have eaten dim sum.
If you're not familiar with it, it's a traditional Cantonese (southern
Chinese) cuisine that is made up of a variety of bite-sized
dishes, usually eaten at breakfast or brunch time and which are
accompanied by tea. Dim sum can be sweet or savoury and can
include steamed dumplings, buns, deep fried squid, tarts,
stuffed pastries, and so on.

Dim sum is actually a *Cantonese* Chinese term, for which the literal
translation in Mandarin Chinese is "diǎnxīn" – yes, that word we've
been using to mean "snack"! However, in order to distinguish just
a general snack from what we know as dim sum – those special
Cantonese bite-sized dishes described above – Mandarin Chinese
speakers will refer to dim sum as "*Cantonese-style* snacks".

"Cantonese-style" is:

广式
guǎng shì
(gwung SHi[8])

Now again, what was "snack" in Chinese?

点心
diǎnxīn
(dee-en-syin)

And as I said just a moment ago, "Cantonese-style" is:

广式
guǎng shì
(gwung SHi)

So how would you say "Cantonese-style snack"?

广式点心
guǎng shì diǎnxīn
(gwung SHi dee-en-syin)

And, as I've just explained, this is how you'll say "dim sum" in Mandarin Chinese.

So how would you say, "I want dim-sum" – literally "I want Cantonese-style snack"?

我要广式点心。
Wǒ yào guǎng shì diǎnxīn.
(wor yow gwung SHi dee-en-syin)

And "you want dim sum"?

你要广式点心。
Nǐ yào guǎng shì diǎnxīn.
(nee yow gwung SHi dee-en-syin)

---

8 Pronounce this "**shi**" like the "**shi**" in "**shi**rt" not the "shi" in "ship". Also, as the SH is in capitals, this tells you that, when you say it, you need to touch your tongue to the roof of your mouth, just as you did with CH and ZH.

"Do you want dim sum?"

你要广式点心吗?
Nǐ yào guǎng shì diǎnxīn ma?
(*nee yow gwung SHi dee-en-syin mah*)

"Do you want a bit of dim sum?"

你要一点广式点心吗?
Nǐ yào yīdiǎn guǎng shì diǎnxīn ma?
(*nee yow ee-dee-en gwung SHi dee-en-syin mah*)

And again, what is "a little more" / "a bit more"?

多一点
duō yīdiǎn
(*dwor ee-dee-en*)

And so how would you say "Do you want a bit more dim sum?"

你要多一点广式点心吗?
Nǐ yào duō yīdiǎn guǎng shì diǎnxīn ma?
(*nee yow dwor ee-dee-en gwung SHi dee-en-syin mah*)

Time to create some words!
Word Building Practice Number 1

Let's forget about whether we want a bit more dim sum for just one moment and instead spend a little time creating some new words.

Now, you may well ask "What do you mean *create* some new words? "Surely that's impossible!"

Well, no, not in Chinese it isn't. This is because Chinese words are frequently made out of other words; they are built out of component parts that can be reused or extracted to *create* new words.

What? Still don't believe me? Okay, I'll show you!

So, from the word creating we just did above, tell me what is "point" in Chinese?

点
diǎn
(dee-en)

And that means both the type of "point" we use in mathematics as well as meaning "point" in the sense of pointing at something. With that in mind, how would you say "I point"?

我点
wǒ diǎn
(wor dee-en)

Now, in fact, when Chinese people order food, they actually talk about pointing at it. After all, originally, when someone ordered, they would simply have pointed at what they wanted. So, not only does "dian" mean both "dot" and "point," it also means "order".

So how would you say "I order" / "I point"?

我点
wǒ diǎn
(wor dee-en)

"I order fried rice"?

我点炒饭。
Wǒ diǎn chǎo fàn.
(wor dee-en CHow fan)

What is "snack"?

点心
diǎnxīn
(dee-en-syin)

And can you remember what "Cantonese-style" was?

广式
guǎng shì
(gwung SHi)

And so how would you say "dim sum" / "Cantonese-style snack"?

广式点心
guǎng shì diǎnxīn
(gwung SHi dee-en-syin)

And what was "I order"?

我点
wǒ diǎn
(wor dee-en)

And so how would you say "I order dim sum"?

我点广式点心。
Wǒ diǎn guǎng shì diǎnxīn.
(wor dee-en gwung SHi dee-en-syin)

How about "I order tea"?

我点茶。
Wǒ diǎn chá.
(wor dee-en CHah)

"I order coffee"?

我点咖啡。
Wǒ diǎn kāfēi.
(wor dee-en kah-fay)

What would be "You order coffee"?

你点咖啡。
Nǐ diǎn kāfēi.
(nee dee-en kah-fay)

And what do you think "He orders coffee" would be?

他点咖啡。
Tā diǎn kāfēi.
(tah dee-en kah-fay)

And "She orders coffee"?

她点咖啡。
Tā diǎn kāfēi.
(tah dee-en kah-fay)

When you want to talk about something in the past in Chinese, it's very easy to do so. For a word like "order", if you want to change it to "ordered", you simply add "le" onto the end of it. I'll show you what I mean. Again, what is "order"?

点
diǎn
(dee-en)

Now add "le" onto the end of this. What do you get?

点了
diǎn le
(dee-en luh)

And that means "ordered".

So how would you say "I ordered"?

我点了
wǒ diǎn le
(*wor dee-en* luh)

And "you ordered"?

你点了
nǐ diǎn le
(*nee dee-en* luh)

"She ordered"?

她点了
tā diǎn le
(tah *dee-en* luh)

How about "She ordered coffee"?

她点了咖啡。
Tā diǎn le kāfēi.
(tah *dee-en* luh kah-fay)

And how about "He ordered tea"?

他点了茶。
Tā diǎn le chá.
(tah *dee-en* luh CHah)

What is "snack" or "a snack"?

点心
diǎnxīn
(*dee-en-syin*)

And what is "Cantonese-style"?

广式
guǎng shì
(*gwung* SHi)

And what is "dim sum"?

广式点心
guǎng shì diǎnxīn
(*gwung SHi dee-en-syin*)

And so how would you say "He ordered dim sum"?

他点了广式点心。
Tā diǎn le guǎng shì diǎnxīn.
(*tah dee-en luh gwung SHi dee-en-syin*)

How about "Did he order dim sum?" – literally "He ordered dim sum ma?"

他点了广式点心吗？
Tā diǎn le guǎng shì diǎnxīn ma?
(*tah dee-en luh gwung SHi dee-en-syin mah*)

Answer this, saying, "I don't know. Maybe."

我不知道。也许。
Wǒ bù zhīdào. yěxǔ.
(*wor boo ZHi-dow. ye-shü*)

Do you remember what "and" is?

和
hé
(*her*)

So how would you say "He ordered tea and dim sum"?

他点了茶和广式点心。
Tā diǎn le chá hé guǎng shì diǎnxīn.
(*tah dee-en luh CHah her gwung SHi dee-en-syin*)

And how would you say "He ordered tea, coffee, and dim sum"?

他点了茶、咖啡和广式点心。
Tā diǎn le chá, kāfēi hé guǎng shì diǎnxīn.
(*tah dee-en luh CHah, kah-fay her gwung SHi dee-en-syin*)

"Pay" in Chinese is:

付
fù
(foo)

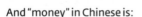

And "money" in Chinese is:

钱
qián
(chee-en[9])

So how would you say "pay money"?

付钱
fù qián
(foo chee-en)

And how about "I pay money"?

我付钱。
Wǒ fù qián.
(wor foo chee-en)

And actually, this is how Chinese people say "I pay", they always specify that they're paying money. So even though in English we don't need to explicitly mention the word "money" when we're talking about paying for something, when we're speaking Chinese, we must include it.

So how would you say "You pay" – literally "You pay money"?

你付钱。
Nǐ fù qián.
(nee foo chee-en)

How about "She pays" / "She pays money"?

她付钱。
Tā fù qián.
(tah foo chee-en)

---

9 Notice how in the pronunciation guidance, the "ch" is small, not in capitals. This tells you that it's just a normal "ch" and therefore you don't need to touch your tongue to the roof of your mouth when you say it.

And "He pays" / "He pays money"?

他付钱。
Tā fù qián.
(tah foo chee-en)

Now once again, what is "order"?

点
diǎn
(dee-en)

And "I order"?

我点
wǒ diǎn
(wor dee-en)

And "I ordered"?

我点了
wǒ diǎn le
(wor dee-en luh)

"I ordered dim sum"?

我点了广式点心。
Wǒ diǎn le guǎng shì diǎnxīn.
(wor dee-en luh gwung SHi dee-en-syin)

And what is "I pay money"?

我付钱。
Wǒ fù qián.
(wor foo chee-en)

Try to say "I paid money".

我付了钱。
Wǒ fù le qián.
(wor foo luh chee-en)

So, just like with how you changed "order" to "ordered" by adding a "le" after "order", so you change "pay money" to "paid money" by adding a "le" after "pay."

How would you say "You paid" / "You paid money"?

你付了钱。
Nǐ fù le qián.
(nee foo luh chee-en)

How about "He paid"?

他付了钱。
Tā fù le qián.
(tah foo luh chee-en)

And "She paid"?

她付了钱。
Tā fù le qián.
(tah foo luh chee-en)

What about "Did she pay?"

她付了钱吗？
Tā fù le qián ma?
(tah foo luh chee-en mah)

"Did you pay?"

你付了钱吗？
Nǐ fù le qián ma?
(nee foo luh chee-en mah)

And going back to where we began, what is "I paid"?

我付了钱。
Wǒ fù le qián.
(wor foo luh chee-en)

And what is "I ordered"?

我点了
wǒ diǎn le
(wor dee-en luh)

"I ordered tea, coffee, and dim sum"?

我点了茶、咖啡和广式点心。
Wǒ diǎn le chá, kāfēi hé guǎng shì diǎnxīn.
(wor dee-en luh CHah, kah-fay her gwung SHi dee-en-syin)

And again, what is "I order"?

我点
wǒ diǎn
(wor dee-en)

"I didn't order" in Chinese is:

我没点
wǒ méi diǎn
(wor may dee-en)

So how would you say "I didn't order tea"?

我没点茶。
Wǒ méi diǎn chá.
(wor may dee-en CHah)

And "I didn't order coffee"?

我没点咖啡。
Wǒ méi diǎn kāfēi.
(wor may dee-en kah-fay)

"You didn't order dim sum"?

你没点广式点心。
Nǐ méi diǎn guǎng shì diǎnxīn.
(nee may dee-en gwung SHi dee-en-syin)

Now again, what is "You pay" – literally "You pay money"?

你付钱。
Nǐ fù qián.
(nee foo chee-en)

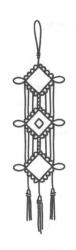

So how do you think you would say "You didn't pay" – literally "You didn't pay money"?

你没付钱。
Nǐ méi fù qián.
(nee may foo chee-en)

How about "I didn't pay"?

我没付钱。
Wǒ méi fù qián.
(wor may foo chee-en)

And "She didn't pay"?

她没付钱。
Tā méi fù qián.
(tah may foo chee-en)

"He didn't pay"?

他没付钱。
Tā méi fù qián.
(tah may foo chee-en)

And again, what is "I order"?

我点
wǒ diǎn
(wor dee-en)

And what is "I ordered"?

我点了
wǒ diǎn le
(wor dee-en luh)

And "he ordered"?

他点了
tā diǎn le
(tah dee-en luh)

"He ordered tea, coffee, and dim sum"?"

他点了茶、咖啡和广式点心。
Tā diǎn le chá, kāfēi hé guǎng shì diǎnxīn.
(tah dee-en luh CHah, kah-fay her gwung SHi dee-en-syin)

And what is "I didn't order"?

我没点
wǒ méi diǎn
(wor may dee-en)

And "I didn't pay"?

我没付钱。
Wǒ méi fù qián.
(wor may foo chee-en)

"But" in Chinese is:

但是
dànshì
(dan-SHi)

So how would you say "…but I didn't pay"?

···但是我没付钱。
…dànshì wǒ méi fù qián.
(dan-SHi wor may foo chee-en)

"…but you didn't pay"?

···但是你没付钱。
…dànshì nǐ méi fù qián.
(dan-SHi nee may foo chee-en)

"…but she didn't pay"?

······但是她没付钱。
…dànshì tā méi fù qián.
(dan-SHi tah may foo chee-en)

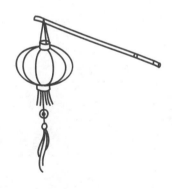

"...but he didn't pay"?

···但是他没付钱。
...dànshì tā méi fù qián.
(dan-SHi tah may foo chee-en)

Now, returning to the sentence we began the chapter with, how would you say "He ordered tea, coffee, and dim sum but he didn't pay"?

他点了茶、咖啡和广式点心，但是他没付钱！
Tā diǎn le chá, kāfēi hé guǎng shì diǎnxīn, dànshì tā méi fù qián!
(tah dee-en luh CHah, kah-fay her gwung SHi dee-en-syin dan-SHi tah may foo chee-en)

Well, you've now worked your way back to the sentence we started with and, although we are only at the end of the second chapter, you are already building long, complex sentences in Chinese and beginning to gain your first insights into how the language works!

Do remember though, if you begin to feel at any point that what you're learning is becoming a bit overwhelming or that it's too much to take in, then simply go back a chapter or two. You should never feel like working through the book is a slog. Instead, just take your time, go at your own pace, and always feel free to repeat part or all of a chapter whenever you need to!

As before, it's time to add some new building blocks to the mix. Again, it will be just six new ones. Here they are:

Once more, these new building blocks have been put into several piles below and what I want you to do is to again make sentences with them, each time using one building block from the first pile, one from the second, one from the third, and one from the fourth. Make as many as you can!

You have now reached your second checklist. Remember, don't skip anything! The checklists are essential if you want what you've learned to remain in your memory for the long term.

So again, cover up the English words on the right-hand side while you read through the list of Chinese words on the left, trying to recall what they mean in English. If you can go through the entire list, giving the correct English meaning for each of the Chinese words / expressions **without making more than 3 mistakes in total**, then you're done. If not, then go through the list again. Keep doing this, either working from the top of the list to the bottom or from the bottom to the top (it doesn't matter which) until you can do it **without making more than 3 mistakes**.

Okay. Ready, set, go!

你 **nǐ** (nee)	you
要 **yào** (yow)	want
你要 **Nǐ yào** (nee yow)	You want
炒 **chǎo** (CHow)	fried
面 **miàn** (mee-en)	noodles
炒面 **chǎo miàn** (CHow mee-en)	fried noodles / chow mein

你要炒面。 **Nǐ yào chǎo miàn.** (nee yow CHow mee-en)	You want fried noodles / chow mein.
豆腐 **dòufu** (doe-foo)	tofu
你要豆腐。 **Nǐ yào dòufu.** (nee yow doe-foo)	You want tofu.
吗？ **ma?** (mah)	spoken question mark
你要豆腐吗？ **Nǐ yào dòufu ma?** (nee yow doe-foo mah)	Do you want tofu?
和 **hé** (her)	and
你要炒面和豆腐吗？ **Nǐ yào chǎo miàn hé dòufu ma?** (nee yow CHow mee-en her doe-foo mah)	Do you want fried noodles and tofu?
饭 **fàn** (fan)	rice
炒饭 **chǎo fàn** (CHow fan)	fried rice
你要炒饭和豆腐吗？ **Nǐ yào chǎo fàn hé dòufu ma?** (nee yow CHow fan her doe-foo mah)	Do you want fried rice and tofu?
不 **bù** (boo)	not
你不要炒饭和豆腐吗？ **Nǐ bù yào chǎo fàn hé dòufu ma?** (nee boo yow CHow fan her doe-foo mah)	Don't you want fried rice and tofu?

我 **wǒ** (wor)	I
我要 **Wǒ yào** (wor yow)	I want
我要炒饭和豆腐。 **Wǒ yào chǎo fàn hé dòufu.** (wor yow CHow fan her doe-foo)	I want fried rice and tofu.
我不要 **Wǒ bù yào** (wor boo yow)	I don't want
我不要炒饭和豆腐。 **Wǒ bù yào chǎo fàn hé dòufu.** (wor boo yow CHow fan her doe-foo)	I don't want fried rice and tofu.
我知道。 **Wǒ zhīdào.** (wor ZHi-dow)	I know.
我知道你要炒面。 **Wǒ zhīdào nǐ yào chǎo miàn.** (wor ZHi-dow nee yow CHow mee-en)	I know you want fried noodles.
我不知道。 **Wǒ bù zhīdào.** (wor boo ZHi-dow)	I don't know.
也许 **yěxǔ** (ye-shü)	maybe
我不知道。也许。 **Wǒ bù zhīdào. Yěxǔ.** (wor boo ZHi-dow. ye-shü)	I don't know. Maybe.
一点 **yīdiǎn** (ee-dee-en)	a little / a bit of
咖啡 **kāfēi** (kah-fay)	coffee

她要 **Tā yào** (tah yow)	She wants
她要一点咖啡。 **Tā yào yīdiǎn kāfēi.** (tah yow *ee-dee-en* kah-fay)	She wants a little coffee.
她要一点咖啡吗？ **Tā yào yīdiǎn kāfēi ma?** (tah yow *ee-dee-en* kah-fay mah)	Does she want a little coffee?
他要 **Tā yào** (tah yow)	He wants
茶 **chá** (CHah)	tea
他要一点茶。 **Tā yào yīdiǎn chá.** (tah yow *ee-dee-en* CHah)	He wants a little tea.
他要一点茶吗？ **Tā yào yīdiǎn chá ma?** (tah yow *ee-dee-en* CHah mah)	Does he want a little tea?
他要一点炒饭吗？ **Tā yào yīdiǎn chǎo fàn ma?** (tah yow *ee-dee-en* CHow fan mah)	Does he want a bit of fried rice?
多一点 **duō yīdiǎn** (dwor *ee-dee-en*)	a bit more / a little more
他要多一点炒饭吗？ **Tā yào duō yīdiǎn chǎo fàn ma?** (tah yow dwor *ee-dee-en* CHow fan mah)	Does he want a bit more fried rice?
可乐 **kělè** (ker-ler)	cola / coke
他要多一点可乐吗？ **Tā yào duō yīdiǎn kělè ma?** (tah yow dwor *ee-dee-en* ker-ler mah)	Does he want a little more coke?

点心 **diǎnxīn** (dee-en-syin)	snack
她要点心。 **Tā yào diǎnxīn.** (tah yow dee-en-syin)	She wants a snack.
广式 **guǎng shì** (gwung SHi)	Cantonese-style
广式点心 **guǎng shì diǎnxīn** (gwung SHi dee-en-syin)	dim sum / Cantonese-style snack
她要广式点心。 **Tā yào guǎng shì diǎnxīn.** (tah yow gwung SHi dee-en-syin)	She wants dim sum.
点 **diǎn** (dee-en)	dot / point / order
我点 **Wǒ diǎn** (wor dee-en)	I order
我点了 **Wǒ diǎn le** (wor dee-en luh)	I ordered
我点了茶、咖啡和广式点心。 **Wǒ diǎn le chá, kāfēi hé guǎng shì diǎnxīn.** (wor dee-en luh CHah, kah-fay her gwung SHi dee-en-syin)	I ordered tea, coffee, and dim sum.
钱 **qián** (chee-en)	money
付钱 **fù qián** (foo chee-en)	pay (literally "pay money")

你付钱 **Nǐ fù qián** (nee foo chee-en)	You pay
你付了钱 **Nǐ fù le qián** (nee foo luh chee-en)	You paid
你付了钱吗？ **Nǐ fù le qián ma?** (nee foo luh chee-en mah)	Did you pay?
没 **méi** (may)	didn't
他没付钱 **Tā méi fù qián** (tah may foo chee-en)	He didn't pay
但是 **dànshì** (dan-SHi)	but
他点了茶、咖啡和广式点心，但是他没付钱！ **Tā diǎn le chá, kāfēi hé guǎng shì diǎnxīn, dànshì tā méi fù qián!** (tah dee-en luh CHah, kah-fay her gwung SHi dee-en-syin dan-SHi tah may foo chee-en)	He ordered tea, coffee, and dim sum but he didn't pay!
他们 **tāmen** (tah-men)	they
披萨 **pīsà** (pee-sa)	pizza
他们点了披萨，但是他们没付钱！ **Tāmen diǎn le pīsà, dànshì tāmen méi fù qián!** (tah-men dee-en luh pee-sa dan-SHi tah-men may foo chee-en)	They ordered pizza but they didn't pay!

吃 **chī** (CH)	eat
他们吃 **Tāmen chī** (tah-men CH)	They eat
他们吃了 **Tāmen chī le** (tah-men CH luh)	They ate
咕噜肉 **gūlū ròu** (goo-loo-roe)	sweet and sour pork
他们吃了咕噜肉。 **Tāmen chī le gūlū ròu.** (tah-men CH luh goo-loo-roe)	They ate sweet and sour pork.
我们 **wǒmen** (wor-men)	we
我们没吃咕噜肉。我们吃了披萨。 **Wǒmen méi chī gūlū ròu. Wǒmen chī le pīsà.** (wor-men may CH goo-loo-roe. Wor-men CH luh pee-sa)	We didn't eat sweet and sour pork. We ate pizza.
买 **mǎi** (my)	buy
我们买了咖啡。 **Wǒmen mǎi le kāfēi.** (wor-men my luh kah-fay)	We bought coffee.
我们买了咖啡。他们买了披萨。 **Wǒmen mǎi le kāfēi. Tāmen mǎi le pīsà.** (wor-men my luh kah-fay. Tah-men my luh pee-sa)	We bought coffee. They bought pizza.

Now, once more, do the same thing again below, except that this time you'll be reading through the list of English words and trying to recall the Chinese. All you need to do is to be able to do one full read-through of them without making **more than 3 mistakes** in total and you're done!

you	你 **nǐ** (nee)
want	要 **yào** (yow)
You want	你要 **Nǐ yào** (nee yow)
fried	炒 **chǎo** (CHow)
noodles	面 **miàn** (mee-en)
fried noodles / chow mein	炒面 **chǎo miàn** (CHow mee-en)
You want fried noodles / chow mein.	你要炒面。 **Nǐ yào chǎo miàn.** (nee yow CHow mee-en)
tofu	豆腐 **dòufu** (doe-foo)
You want tofu.	你要豆腐。 **Nǐ yào dòufu.** (nee yow doe-foo)
spoken question mark	吗？ **ma?** (mah)

Do you want tofu?	你要豆腐吗？ **Nǐ yào dòufu ma?** (nee yow doe-foo mah)
and	和 **hé** (her)
Do you want fried noodles and tofu?	你要炒面和豆腐吗？ **Nǐ yào chǎo miàn hé dòufu ma?** (nee yow CHow mee-en her doe-foo mah)
rice	饭 **fàn** (fan)
fried rice	炒饭 **chǎo fàn** (CHow fan)
Do you want fried rice and tofu?	你要炒饭和豆腐吗？ **Nǐ yào chǎo fàn hé dòufu ma?** (nee yow CHow fan her doe-foo mah)
not	不 **bù** (boo)
Don't you want fried rice and tofu?	你不要炒饭和豆腐吗？ **Nǐ bù yào chǎo fàn hé dòufu ma?** (nee boo yow CHow fan her doe-foo mah)
I	我 **wǒ** (wor)
I want	我要 **Wǒ yào** (wor yow)
I want fried rice and tofu.	我要炒饭和豆腐。 **Wǒ yào chǎo fàn hé dòufu.** (wor yow CHow fan her doe-foo)
I don't want	我不要 **Wǒ bù yào** (wor boo yow)

I don't want fried rice and tofu.	我不要炒饭和豆腐。 **Wǒ bù yào chǎo fàn hé dòufu.** (wor boo yow CHow fan her *doe*-foo)
I know.	我知道。 **Wǒ zhīdào.** (wor ZHi-dow)
I know you want fried noodles.	我知道你要炒面。 **Wǒ zhīdào nǐ yào chǎo miàn.** (wor ZHi-dow nee yow CHow mee-en)
I don't know.	我不知道。 **Wǒ bù zhīdào.** (wor boo ZHi-dow)
maybe	也许 **yěxǔ** (ye-shü)
I don't know. Maybe.	我不知道。也许。 **Wǒ bù zhīdào. Yěxǔ.** (wor boo ZHi-dow. ye-shü)
a little / a bit of	一点 **yīdiǎn** (ee-dee-en)
coffee	咖啡 **kāfēi** (kah-fay)
She wants	她要 **Tā yào** (tah yow)
She wants a little coffee.	她要一点咖啡。 **Tā yào yīdiǎn kāfēi.** (tah yow ee-dee-en kah-fay)
Does she want a little coffee?	她要一点咖啡吗？ **Tā yào yīdiǎn kāfēi ma?** (tah yow ee-dee-en kah-fay mah)
He wants	他要 **Tā yào** (tah yow)

tea	茶 **chá** (CHah)
He wants a little tea.	他要一点茶。 **Tā yào yīdiǎn chá.** (tah yow ee-dee-en CHah)
Does he want a little tea?	他要一点茶吗？ **Tā yào yīdiǎn chá ma?** (tah yow ee-dee-en CHah mah)
Does he want a bit of fried rice?	他要一点炒饭吗？ **Tā yào yīdiǎn chǎo fàn ma?** (tah yow ee-dee-en CHow fan mah)
a bit more / a little more	多一点 **duō yīdiǎn** (dwor ee-dee-en)
Does he want a bit more fried rice?	他要多一点炒饭吗？ **Tā yào duō yīdiǎn chǎo fàn ma?** (tah yow dwor ee-dee-en CHow fan mah)
cola / coke	可乐 **kělè** (ker-ler)
Does he want a little more coke?	他要多一点可乐吗？ **Tā yào duō yīdiǎn kělè ma?** (tah yow dwor ee-dee-en ker-ler mah)
snack	点心 **diǎnxīn** (dee-en-syin)
She wants a snack.	她要点心。 **Tā yào diǎnxīn.** (tah yow dee-en-syin)
Cantonese-style	广式 **guǎng shì** (gwung SHi)
dim sum / Cantonese-style snack	广式点心 **guǎng shì diǎnxīn** (gwung SHi dee-en-syin)

She wants dim sum.	她要广式点心。 **Tā yào guǎng shì diǎnxīn.** (tah yow gwung SHi dee-en-syin)
dot / point / order	点 **diǎn** (dee-en)
I order	我点 **Wǒ diǎn** (wor dee-en)
I ordered	我点了 **Wǒ diǎn le** (wor dee-en luh)
I ordered tea, coffee, and dim sum.	我点了茶、咖啡和广式点心。 **Wǒ diǎn le chá, kāfēi hé guǎng shì diǎnxīn.** (wor dee-en luh CHah, kah-fay her gwung SHi dee-en-syin)
money	钱 **qián** (chee-en)
pay (literally "pay money")	付钱 **fù qián** (foo chee-en)
You pay	你付钱 **Nǐ fù qián** (nee foo chee-en)
You paid	你付了钱 **Nǐ fù le qián** (nee foo luh chee-en)
Did you pay?	你付了钱吗？ **Nǐ fù le qián ma?** (nee foo luh chee-en mah)
didn't	没 **méi** (may)

He didn't pay	他没付钱 **Tā méi fù qián** (tah may foo chee-en)
but	但是 **dànshì** (dan-SHi)
He ordered tea, coffee, and dim sum but he didn't pay!	他点了茶、咖啡和广式点心，但是他没付钱！ **Tā diǎn le chá, kāfēi hé guǎng shì diǎnxīn, dànshì tā méi fù qián!** (tah dee-en luh CHah, kah-fay her gwung SHi dee-en-syin dan-SHi tah may foo chee-en)
they	他们 **tāmen** (tah-men)
pizza	披萨 **pīsà** (pee-sa)
They ordered pizza but they didn't pay!	他们点了披萨，但是他们没付钱！ **Tāmen diǎn le pīsà, dànshì tāmen méi fù qián!** (tah-men dee-en luh pee-sa dan-SHi tah-men may foo chee-en)
eat	吃 **chī** (CH)
They eat	他们吃 **Tāmen chī** (tah-men CH)
They ate	他们吃了 **Tāmen chī le** (tah-men CH luh)
sweet and sour pork	咕噜肉 **gūlū ròu** (goo-loo-roe)

They ate sweet and sour pork.	他们吃了咕噜肉。 **Tāmen chī le gūlū ròu.** (tah-men CH luh *goo-loo-roe*)
we	我们 **wǒmen** (wor-men)
We didn't eat sweet and sour pork. We ate pizza.	我们没吃咕噜肉。我们吃了 披萨。 **Wǒmen méi chī gūlū ròu. Wǒmen chī le pīsà.** (wor-men may CH *goo-loo-roe.* Wor-men CH luh *pee-sa*)
buy	买 **mǎi** (my)
We bought coffee.	我们买了咖啡。 **Wǒmen mǎi le kāfēi.** (wor-men my luh kah-fay)
We bought coffee. They bought pizza.	我们买了咖啡。他们买了披 萨。 **Wǒmen mǎi le kāfēi. Tāmen mǎi le pīsà.** (wor-men my luh kah-fay. Tah-men my luh *pee-sa*)

Well, that's it, you're done with Chapter 2! Remember, don't try to hold on to or remember anything you've learned here. Everything you learn in earlier chapters will be brought back up and reinforced in later chapters. You don't need to do anything or make any effort to memorise anything. The book has been organised in such a way that it will do that for you. So, off you go now and have a rest please!

Stop while you're still enjoying it!

Arnold Schwarzenegger once said that the key to his body-building success was that he stopped his workout each day just *before* it started to get boring. On the few occasions that he went past that point, he found it incredibly hard to return to the gym again the next day – and he *loved* working out.

So, as you will almost certainly recall, Tip 1 suggested that you should study every day – which you definitely should do if you can. But that doesn't mean that you should overdo it. So, if you're not really in the mood, just do 5 minutes. If you are in the mood though, don't push yourself too hard. Stop before you get to the point where it doesn't feel fun any longer. Best to leave yourself feeling hungry for more rather than bloated and fed up!

CHAPTER 3

We went to Shanghai and played mahjong — I don't know where my money went...

"We went to Shanghai and played mahjong." This sentence doesn't seem especially complicated in English and yet, even if you've studied Chinese before, you might well find it impossible to know where to begin in order to say this in Mandarin. By the end of this chapter, however, you will have learned how to build this sentence, plus a great deal of other Chinese words and expressions besides.

Let's begin!

Once again, how would you say "I order"?

我点
wǒ diǎn
(wor dee-en)

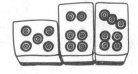

How about "I ordered"?

我点了
wǒ diǎn le
(wor dee-en luh)

Do you remember what "buy" was from the most recent building block section?

买
mǎi
(my[10])

So how would you say "I buy"?

我买
wǒ mǎi
(wor my)

~~~~~~~~~~~~~~~~
10   Pronounced more or less just like the English word "my".

How about "we buy"?

我们买
wǒmen mǎi
(wor-men my)

And "he buys"?

他买
tā mǎi
(tah my)

What about "she buys"?

她买
tā mǎi
(tah my)

Do you think you can work out how to say "she *bought*"?

她买了
tā mǎi le
(tah my luh)

"She bought dim sum"?

她买了广式点心。
Tā mǎi le guǎng shì diǎnxīn.
(tah my luh gwung SHi dee-en-syin)

What is "cola" / "coke"?

可乐
kělè
(ker-ler)

And so how would you say "She bought coke"?

她买了可乐。
Tā mǎi le kělè.
(tah my luh ker-ler)

What is "pizza"?

披萨
pīsà
(pee-sa)

And so what would be "She bought pizza and coke"?

她买了披萨和可乐。
Tā mǎi le pīsà hé kělè.
(tah my luh pee-sa her ker-ler)

Can you remember from the building blocks section what "sweet and sour pork" is?

咕噜肉
gūlū ròu
(goo-loo-roe)

So how would you say "She bought sweet and sour pork"?

她买了咕噜肉。
Tā mǎi le gūlū ròu.
(tah my luh goo-loo-roe)

How about "She ordered sweet and sour pork"?

她点了咕噜肉。
Tā diǎn le gūlū ròu.
(tah dee-en luh goo-loo-roe)

What is "eat"?

吃
chī
(CH)

And "I eat"?

我吃
wǒ chī
(wor CH)

How about "she eats"?

她吃
tā chī
(tah CH)

"He eats"?

他吃
tā chī
(tah CH)

"They eat"?

他们吃
tāmen chī
(tah-men CH)

And so how do you think you would say "they ate"?

他们吃了
tāmen chī le
(tah-men CH luh)

How about "They ate sweet and sour pork"?

他们吃了咕噜肉。
Tāmen chī le gūlū ròu.
(tah-men CH luh *goo-loo-roe*)

And "They ate dim sum and sweet and sour pork"?

他们吃了广式点心和咕噜肉。
Tāmen chī le guǎng shì diǎnxīn hé gūlū ròu.
(tah-men CH luh *gwung* SHi *dee-en-syin* her *goo-loo-roe*)

"Go" in Chinese is:

去
qù
(chü[11])

11　Another word with an "ü" sound. To say "chü" correctly, round your lips and say "chee" **while keeping your lips rounded**.

So how would you say "they go"?

他们去
tāmen qù
(tah-men chü)

How about "I go"?

我去
wǒ qù
(wor chü)

And "you go"?

你去
nǐ qù
(nee chü)

What about "he goes"?

他去
tā qù
(tah chü)

And "she goes"?

她去
tā qù
(tah chü)

Do you think you can work out how you would say "she went"?

她去了
tā qù le
(tah chü luh)

So just as we transformed "order" into "ordered" and "eat" into " ate" by adding "le", we have now changed "go" into "went" in exactly the same way.

So how would you say "he went"?

他去了
tā qù le
(tah chü luh)

And "I went"?

我去了
wǒ qù le
(wor chü luh)

And actually, this means both "I went" and "I went to" – there's no difference between them in Chinese.

"Shanghai" in Chinese is, of course,:

上海
Shànghǎi
(SHanghai[12])

Now, once again, what is "I go"?

我去
wǒ qù
(wor chü)

And what is "I went" or "I went to"?

我去了
wǒ qù le
(wor chü luh)

So how would you say "I went to Shanghai"?

我去了上海。
Wǒ qù le Shànghǎi.
(wor chü luh SHanghai)

---

12   There's no need for too much special guidance on how to pronounce "Shanghai" in Chinese, as there is little difference between the English and Chinese pronunciation. Just make sure to pronounce the SH at the beginning with your tongue touched to the roof of your mouth and you'll be fine!

And "She went to Shanghai"?

她去了上海。
Tā qù le Shànghǎi.
(tah chü luh SHanghai)

What about "He went to Shanghai"?

他去了上海。
Tā qù le Shànghǎi.
(tah chü luh SHanghai)

And how do you think you would say "He went to Beijing"?

他去了北京。
Tā qù le Běijīng.
(tah chü luh bay-jing)

What is "but"?

但是
dànshì
(dan-SHi)

And so how would you say "…but he went to Beijing"?

…但是他去了北京。
…**dànshì tā qù le Běijīng.**
(dan-SHi tah chü luh bay-jing)

And what about "I went to Shanghai but he went to Beijing"?

我去了上海，但是他去了北京。
Wǒ qù le Shànghǎi, dànshì tā qù le Běijīng.
(wor chü luh SHanghai dan-SHi tah chü luh bay-jing)

What is "we"?

我们
wǒmen
(wor-men)

"We went to Beijing"?

我们去了北京。
Wǒmen qù le Běijīng.
(wor-men chü luh bay-jing)

"Hit" in Chinese is:

打
dǎ
(dah)

So how would you say "we hit"?

我们打
wǒmen dǎ
(wor-men dah)

"Mahjong" in Mandarin Chinese is:

麻将
májiàng
(mah-jang)

Now again, what was "we hit"?

我们打
wǒmen dǎ
(wor-men dah)

And what was "mahjong"?

麻将
májiàng
(mah-jang)

And so how would you say "We hit mahjong"?

我们打麻将。
Wǒmen dǎ májiàng.
(wor-men dah mah-jang)

And this is how you would say "we play mahjong" in Chinese. Just think of the way the mahjong tiles *hit* the table when you put them down and it will begin to make sense to you as to why Chinese speakers express the idea of playing mahjong in this way.

So, how would you say "I play mahjong" / "I hit mahjong"?

我打麻将。
Wǒ dǎ májiàng.
(*wor dah mah-jang*)

And "They play mahjong"?

他们打麻将。
Tāmen dǎ májiàng.
(*tah-men dah mah-jang*)

And how would you say "They play*ed* mahjong"?

他们打了麻将。
Tāmen dǎ le májiàng.
(*tah-men dah luh mah-jang*)

How about "You played mahjong"?

你打了麻将。
Nǐ dǎ le májiàng.
(*nee dah luh mah-jang*)

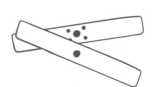

What is the spoken question mark?

吗
ma
(*mah*)

Add that onto the end of the sentence now and ask "Did you play mahjong?" – literally "You played mahjong ma?"

你打了麻将吗？
Nǐ dǎ le májiàng ma?
(*nee dah luh mah-jang mah*)

How about "Did he play mahjong?"

他打了麻将吗？
Tā dǎ le májiàng ma?
(tah dah luh mah-jang mah)

And "Did she play mahjong?"

她打了麻将吗？
Tā dǎ le májiàng ma?
(tah dah luh mah-jang mah)

Now again, what were "fried noodles" / "chow mein"?

炒面
chǎo miàn
(CHow mee-en)

And what was "fried rice"?

炒饭
chǎo fàn
(CHow fan)

And what was "and"?

和
hé
(her)

And so how would you say "fried noodles *and* fried rice"?

炒面和炒饭
chǎo miàn hé chǎo fàn
(CHow mee-en her CHow fan)

What is "tea"?

茶
chá
(CHah)

And what is "coffee"?

咖啡
kāfēi
(kah-fay)

So how would you say "tea and coffee"?

茶和咖啡
chá hé kāfēi
(CHah her kah-fay)

So, we are definitely very familiar with the word for "and" in Chinese. However, you'll find it does not work in *exactly* the same way as "and" does in English. I'll show you what I mean.

Again, how would say "tea and coffee"?

茶和咖啡
chá hé kāfēi
(CHah her kah-fay)

And how would you say "fried noodles and fried rice"?

炒面和炒饭
chǎo miàn hé chǎo fàn
(CHow mee-en her CHow fan)

So, we've just used "and" (hé) to connect two things, two items – two types of food in the last example – in Chinese, which is, of course, something we also do in English.

However, in English, as well as using "and" to join two items together, we also use it to join two halves of a sentence together. For instance, we'll say "I went to Beijing *and* I ordered fried noodles". Or "I got married *and* I had two children." So, in English we very often take two halves of a sentence and join them together using "and". In Chinese, however, they don't bother to do this.

Now, you may ask, "Well, what do they do instead?" And the answer to this is: they do nothing. Again, I'll show you what I mean.

What is "I go"?

我去
wǒ qù
(wor chü)

And what is "I went"?

我去了
wǒ qù le
(wor chü luh)

And how would you say "I went to Shanghai"?

我去了上海。
Wǒ qù le Shànghǎi.
(wor chü luh SHanghai)

What is "I order"?

我点
wǒ diǎn
(wor dee-en)

And what is "I ordered"?

我点了
wǒ diǎn le
(wor dee-en luh)

And how would you say "I ordered fried noodles"?

我点了炒面。
Wǒ diǎn le chǎo miàn.
(wor dee-en luh CHow mee-en)

Now if you want you to say "I went to Shanghai *and* ordered fried noodles", you won't bother including the "and" because you simply don't need it in Chinese. You can just skip it.

So say now "I went to Shanghai and ordered fried noodles", which in Chinese will literally be: "I went to Shanghai, ordered fried noodles." How would you say that?

我去了上海，点了炒面。
Wǒ qù le Shànghǎi, diǎn le chǎo miàn.
(wor chü luh SHanghai, dee-en luh CHow mee-en)

How about "I went to Beijing and ordered fried noodles"?

我去了北京，点了炒面。
Wǒ qù le Běijīng, diǎn le chǎo miàn.
(wor chü luh bay-jing, dee-en luh CHow mee-en)

So the sentence is exactly the same as in English, except that it's missing the "and". This is because, as I've said, in Chinese you only need to use "and" to connect two items, two things.

For example, how would you say "fried noodles *and* fried rice"?

炒面和炒饭
chǎo miàn hé chǎo fàn
(CHow mee-en her CHow fan)

So, we're connecting two items here, so we include the "and".

But how would you say "I went to Beijing *and* ordered fried noodles"?

我去了北京，点了炒面。
Wǒ qù le Běijīng, diǎn le chǎo miàn.
(wor chü luh bay-jing, dee-en luh CHow mee-en)

So, we're connecting two halves of a sentence here, therefore we don't bother to include the "and".

Try this one: "I went to Beijing *and* ordered fried noodles *and* fried rice."

我去了北京，点了炒面和炒饭。
Wǒ qù le Běijīng, diǎn le chǎo miàn hé chǎo fàn.
(wor chü luh bay-jing, dee-en luh CHow mee-en her CHow fan)

So here, in this sentence, we've connected the two items using "and" (the fried noodles *and* fried rice) but we didn't use an "and" to connect the two halves of the sentence together. And that's because, in Chinese, we only use "and" to join two things together – we don't use it to connect two halves of a sentence together, instead we just skip it!

Let's try another example.

What is "I play mahjong" – literally "I hit mahjong"?

我打麻将。
Wǒ dǎ májiàng.
(wor dah mah-jang)

And how would you say "I played mahjong"?

我打了麻将。
Wǒ dǎ le májiàng.
(wor dah luh mah-jang)

And so how would you say "I went to Beijing and played mahjong"?

我去了北京、打了麻将。
Wǒ qù le Běijīng, dǎ le májiàng.
(wor chü luh bay-jing, dah luh mah-jang)

And how about "I went to Shanghai and played mahjong"?

我去了上海、打了麻将。
Wǒ qù le Shànghǎi, dǎ le májiàng.
(wor chü luh SHanghai, dah luh mah-jang)

What about "We went to Shanghai and played mahjong"?

我们去了上海、打了麻将。
Wǒmen qù le Shànghǎi, dǎ le májiàng.
(wor-men chü luh SHanghai, dah luh mah-jang)

Do you remember how to say "I pay" – literally "I pay money"?

我付钱。
Wǒ fù qián.
(wor foo chee-en)

And "I paid" / "I paid money"?

我付了钱。
Wǒ fù le qián.
(wor foo luh chee-en)

Now, which part of that means "money"?

钱
qián
(*chee-en*)

And what is "I"?

我
wǒ
(*wor*)

"My" in Chinese is:

我的
wǒde
(*wor-duh*[13])

Notice here that to make the word "my" we've simply taken the Chinese word for "I" (**wǒ**) and added "de" onto the end of it, giving us "**wǒde**" meaning "my".

So how would you say "my money"?

我的钱
wǒde qián
(*wor-duh chee-en*)

And how would you say "my tea"?

我的茶
wǒde chá
(*wor-duh CHah*)

And "my coffee"?

我的咖啡
wǒde kāfēi
(*wor-duh kah-fay*)

13　The pronunciation of the "de" part is the same as the sound the letter "d" makes in English. It's that sound that people say when they're first teaching a child how to read and they tell the child that "D makes a 'duh' sound." So, to say "my" you pronounce the "I" / "wǒ" as "wor" just as you usually do, and then add that little "duh" sound immediately afterwards.

What is "you"?

你
nǐ
(nee)

And again, what was "I"?

我
wǒ
(wor)

And what did we add onto the end of "I" to turn it into "my"?

的
de
(duh)

So now try adding this same "de" onto the end of "you" (nǐ). Doing that, what do you get?

你的
nǐde
(nee-duh)

And this means "your".

So once more, what is "I"?

我
wǒ
(wor)

And what is "my"?

我的
wǒde
(wor-duh)

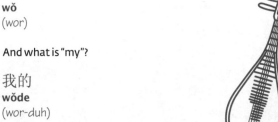

And what is "you"?

你
nǐ
(nee)

And what is "your"?

你的
nǐde
(nee-duh)

And so how would you say "your coffee"?

你的咖啡
nǐde kāfēi
(nee-duh kah-fay)

And "your tea"?

你的茶
nǐde chá
(nee-duh CHah)

"Your money"?

你的钱
nǐde qián
(nee-duh chee-en)

And how about "my money"?

我的钱
wǒde qián
(wor-duh chee-en)

And what is "I go"?

我去
wǒ qù
(wor chü)

And so what is "I went"?

我去了
wǒ qù le
(wor chü luh)

How about "he went"?

他去了
tā qù le
(tah chü luh)

And so, just on its own, what is "went"?

去了
qù le
(chü luh)

And so how do you think you would say "my money went"?

我的钱去了
wǒde qián qù le
(wor-duh chee-en chü luh)

"Where" in Chinese is:

哪里
nǎlǐ
(nah-lee)

So how would you say, literally, "My money went where?"

我的钱去了哪里？
Wǒde qián qù le nǎlǐ?
(wor-duh chee-en chü luh nah-lee)

And this is how you'd say "Where did my money go?"
or "Where's my money gone?" in Chinese.

Now again, what is "your"?

你的
nǐde
(nee-duh)

And "your money"?

你的钱
nǐde qián
(nee-duh chee-en)

And so how would you say "your money went"?

你的钱去了
nǐde qián qù le
(nee-duh chee-en chü luh)

"Where", as I've already mentioned, is of course:

哪里
nǎlǐ
(nah-lee)

So how would you say "Where did your money go?" – literally "Your money went where?"

你的钱去了哪里？
Nǐde qián qù le nǎlǐ?
(nee-duh chee-en chü luh nah-lee)

And how would you say "Where did your coffee go?"

你的咖啡去了哪里？
Nǐde kāfēi qù le nǎlǐ?
(nee-duh kah-fay chü luh nah-lee)

And "Where did your tea go?"

你的茶去了哪里？
Nǐde chá qù le nǎlǐ?
(nee-duh CHah chü luh nah-lee)

How about "Where did my tea go?"

我的茶去了哪里？
Wǒde chá qù le nǎlǐ?
(wor-duh CHah chü luh nah-lee)

And "Where did my money go?"

我的钱去了哪里？
Wǒde qián qù le nǎlǐ?
(wor-duh chee-en chü luh nah-lee)

What is "I know"?

我知道。
Wǒ zhīdào.
(wor ZHi-dow)

And what is "not"?

不
bù
(boo)

So how would you say "I don't know"?

我不知道。
Wǒ bù zhīdào.
(wor boo ZHi-dow)

And again, how would you say "Where did my money go?" / "My money went where?"

我的钱去了哪里？
Wǒde qián qù le nǎlǐ?
(wor-duh chee-en chü luh nah-lee)

If you want to say "I don't know where my money went", it's very simple.
You'll simply say "I don't know my money went where."

So again, what is "I know"?

我知道。
Wǒ zhīdào.
(wor ZHi-dow)

And "I don't know"?

我不知道。
Wǒ bù zhīdào.
(wor boo ZHi-dow)

And what is "My money went where?"

我的钱去了哪里？
Wǒde qián qù le nǎlǐ?
(wor-duh chee-en chü luh nah-lee)

Now put these together and say "I don't know where my money went" – literally "I don't know my money went where".

我不知道我的钱去了哪里。
Wǒ bù zhīdào wǒde qián qù le nǎlǐ.
(wor boo ZHi-dow wor-duh chee-en chü luh nah-lee)

What is "your"?

你的
nǐde
(nee-duh)

And so how would you say "I don't know where your money went" – literally "I don't know your money went where".

我不知道你的钱去了哪里。
Wǒ bù zhīdào nǐde qián qù le nǎlǐ.
(wor boo ZHi-dow nee-duh chee-en chü luh nah-lee)

What is "I went to Shanghai"?

我去了上海。
Wǒ qù le Shànghǎi.
(wor chü luh SHanghai)

And how would you say "I played mahjong"?

我打了麻将。
Wǒ dǎ le májiàng.
(wor dah luh mah-jang)

And so how would you say "I went to Shanghai and played mahjong"?

我去了上海，打了麻将。
Wǒ qù le Shànghǎi, dǎ le májiàng.
(wor chü luh SHanghai, dah luh mah-jang)

When you said that, did you remember that you don't need an "and" to join two halves of a sentence together in Chinese? That instead you just skip it? If not, don't worry. The more you practise building sentences, the more these rules will simply become instinctive – you'll just know what sounds right. Now, let's get back to those sentences.

How would you say "We went to Shanghai and played mahjong"?

我们去了上海，打了麻将。
Wǒmen qù le Shànghǎi, dǎ le májiàng.
(wor-men chü luh SHanghai, dah luh mah-jang)

And what is "I know"?

我知道。
Wǒ zhīdào.
(wor ZHi-dow)

And "I don't know"?

我不知道。
Wǒ bù zhīdào.
(wor boo ZHi-dow)

And again, what is "my money"?

我的钱
wǒde qián
(wor-duh chee-en)

And again how would you say "my money went"?

我的钱去了
wǒde qián qù le
(wor-duh chee-en chü luh)

And what is "where"?

哪里
nǎlǐ
(nah-lee)

And so how would you say "Where did my money go?" / "My money went where?"

我的钱去了哪里？
Wǒde qián qù le nǎlǐ?
(wor-duh chee-en chü luh nah-lee)

And how would you say "I don't know where my money went" – literally "I don't know my money went where"?

我不知道我的钱去了哪里。
Wǒ bù zhīdào wǒde qián qù le nǎlǐ.
(wor boo ZHi-dow wor-duh chee-en chü luh nah-lee)

Now, put all this together and (taking your time to think it out) say "We went to Shanghai and played mahjong – I don't know where my money went…"

我们去了上海，打了麻将 – 我不知道我的钱去了哪里！
Wǒmen qù le Shànghǎi, dǎ le májiàng – wǒ bù zhīdào wǒde qián qù le nǎlǐ!
(wor-men chü luh SHanghai, dah luh mah-jang – wor boo ZHi-dow wor-duh chee-en chü luh nah-lee)

How did you find that final, complex sentence? Try it a few more times, even if you got it right, until you feel comfortable constructing it. Every time you practise building these long sentences, the naturalness and fluidity of your spoken Chinese will improve and your confidence levels in speaking the language will rise along with it.

Building Blocks 3

It's time again to add some new building blocks. Here they are:

太极
tàijí
(ty-jee[14])
tai chi

你们
nimen[15]
(nee-men)
you (MTOP)

中文
Zhōngwén[16]
(ZHong-wen)
Chinese

功夫
gōng fū
(gong foo)
kung fu

学了
xué le
(shüwair luh)
learned / studied

英文
Yīngwén[17]
(ying-wen)
English

So, you've got your new building blocks. Make as many sentences as you can!

14 Pronounce this "ty" just like the "ty" in the English word "type".

15 You've already learned a word for "you" in Chinese: nǐ. Nǐ is used for talking to one person. When you're using "you" to refer to more than one person in Chinese, however, you'll use nǐmen. From now on, whenever you see "you" written in English in the book, if it has MTOP (which stands for "more than one person") written afterwards then you should use nǐmen to translate the English word "you". If there's no MTOP though, just use nǐ!

16 Zhōngwén literally means "middle language" as China was thought of by the ancient Chinese as being in the middle of the world, as being the "middle country" at the centre of world events; therefore the language spoken there was logically considered to be the middle language.

17 Yīngwén literally means "brave language". It takes its name from the Chinese term for Britain – Yīngguó – which means "brave country". And that's probably a good description, considering the weather we have to put up with.

107

You know what to do with the checklist now, so you don't need any reminding about that.

Do bear one thing in mind though. The checklists don't need to be done in one sitting. So, if you get through a page or two and feel that's enough then simply leave the rest until the next day. Always work at your own pace and don't do so much that you end up feeling overwhelmed. "Steady as she goes" should be your mantra!

你 **nǐ** (nee)	you
要 **yào** (yow)	want
你要 **Nǐ yào** (nee yow)	You want
炒 **chǎo** (CHow)	fried
面 **miàn** (mee-en)	noodles
炒面 **chǎo miàn** (CHow mee-en)	fried noodles / chow mein
你要炒面。 **Nǐ yào chǎo miàn.** (nee yow CHow mee-en)	You want fried noodles / chow mein.
豆腐 **dòufu** (doe-foo)	tofu
你要豆腐。 **Nǐ yào dòufu.** (nee yow doe-foo)	You want tofu.

吗？ **ma?** (mah)	spoken question mark
你要豆腐吗？ **Nǐ yào dòufu ma?** (nee yow *doe-foo* mah)	Do you want tofu?
和 **hé** (her)	and
你要炒面和豆腐吗？ **Nǐ yào chǎo miàn hé dòufu ma?** (nee yow CHow mee-en her *doe-foo* mah)	Do you want fried noodles and tofu?
饭 **fàn** (fan)	rice
炒饭 **chǎo fàn** (CHow fan)	fried rice
你要炒饭和豆腐吗？ **Nǐ yào chǎo fàn hé dòufu ma?** (nee yow CHow fan her *doe-foo* mah)	Do you want fried rice and tofu?
不 **bù** (boo)	not
你不要炒饭和豆腐吗？ **Nǐ bù yào chǎo fàn hé dòufu ma?** (nee boo yow CHow fan her *doe-foo* mah)	Don't you want fried rice and tofu?
我 **wǒ** (wor)	I
我要 **Wǒ yào** (wor yow)	I want
我要炒饭和豆腐。 **Wǒ yào chǎo fàn hé dòufu.** (wor yow CHow fan her *doe-foo*)	I want fried rice and tofu.

我不要 **Wǒ bù yào** (wor boo yow)	I don't want
我不要炒饭和豆腐。 **Wǒ bù yào chǎo fàn hé dòufu.** (wor boo yow CHow fan her doe-foo)	I don't want fried rice and tofu.
我知道。 **Wǒ zhīdào.** (wor ZHi-dow)	I know.
我知道你要炒面。 **Wǒ zhīdào nǐ yào chǎo miàn.** (wor ZHi-dow nee yow CHow mee-en)	I know you want fried noodles.
我不知道。 **Wǒ bù zhīdào.** (wor boo ZHi-dow)	I don't know.
也许 **yěxǔ** (ye-shü)	maybe
我不知道。也许。 **Wǒ bù zhīdào. Yěxǔ.** (wor boo ZHi-dow. ye-shü)	I don't know. Maybe.
一点 **yīdiǎn** (ee-dee-en)	a little / a bit of
咖啡 **kāfēi** (kah-fay)	coffee
她要 **Tā yào** (tah yow)	She wants
她要一点咖啡。 **Tā yào yīdiǎn kāfēi.** (tah yow ee-dee-en kah-fay)	She wants a little coffee.
她要一点咖啡吗？ **Tā yào yīdiǎn kāfēi ma?** (tah yow ee-dee-en kah-fay mah)	Does she want a little coffee?

他要 **Tā yào** (tah yow)	He wants
茶 **chá** (CHah)	tea
他要一点茶。 **Tā yào yīdiǎn chá.** (tah yow ee-dee-en CHah)	He wants a little tea.
他要一点茶吗？ **Tā yào yīdiǎn chá ma?** (tah yow ee-dee-en CHah mah)	Does he want a little tea?
他要一点炒饭吗？ **Tā yào yīdiǎn chǎo fàn ma?** (tah yow ee-dee-en CHow fan mah)	Does he want a bit of fried rice?
多一点 **duō yīdiǎn** (dwor ee-dee-en)	a bit more / a little more
他要多一点炒饭吗？ **Tā yào duō yīdiǎn chǎo fàn ma?** (tah yow dwor ee-dee-en CHow fan mah)	Does he want a bit more fried rice?
可乐 **kělè** (ker-ler)	cola / coke
他要多一点可乐吗？ **Tā yào duō yīdiǎn kělè ma?** (tah yow dwor ee-dee-en ker-ler mah)	Does he want a little more coke?
点心 **diǎnxīn** (dee-en-syin)	snack
她要点心。 **Tā yào diǎnxīn.** (tah yow dee-en-syin)	She wants a snack.
广式 **guǎng shì** (gwung SHi)	Cantonese-style

广式点心 **guǎng shì diǎnxīn** (gwung SHi dee-en-syin)	dim sum / Cantonese-style snack
她要广式点心。 **Tā yào guǎng shì diǎnxīn.** (tah yow gwung SHi dee-en-syin)	She wants dim sum.
点 **diǎn** (dee-en)	dot / point / order
我点 **Wǒ diǎn** (wor dee-en)	I order
我点了 **Wǒ diǎn le** (wor dee-en luh)	I ordered
我点了茶、咖啡和广式点心。 **Wǒ diǎn le chá, kāfēi hé guǎng shì diǎnxīn.** (wor dee-en luh CHah, kah-fay her gwung SHi dee-en-syin)	I ordered tea, coffee, and dim sum.
钱 **qián** (chee-en)	money
付钱 **fù qián** (foo chee-en)	pay (literally "pay money")
你付钱 **Nǐ fù qián** (nee foo chee-en)	You pay
你付了钱 **Nǐ fù le qián** (nee foo luh chee-en)	You paid
你付了钱吗？ **Nǐ fù le qián ma?** (nee foo luh chee-en mah)	Did you pay?

没 **méi** (may)	didn't
他没付钱 **Tā méi fù qián** (tah may foo chee-en)	He didn't pay
但是 **dànshì** (dan-SHi)	but
他点了茶、咖啡和广式点心，但是他没付钱！ **Tā diǎn le chá, kāfēi hé guǎng shì diǎnxīn, dànshì tā méi fù qián!** (tah dee-en luh CHah, kah-fay her gwung SHi dee-en-syin dan-SHi tah may foo chee-en)	He ordered tea, coffee, and dim sum but he didn't pay!
他们 **tāmen** (tah-men)	they
披萨 **pīsà** (pee-sa)	pizza
他们点了披萨，但是他们没付钱！ **Tāmen diǎn le pīsà, dànshì tāmen méi fù qián!** (tah-men dee-en luh pee-sa dan-SHi tah-men may foo chee-en)	They ordered pizza but they didn't pay!
吃 **chī** (CH)	eat
他们吃 **Tāmen chī** (tah-men CH)	They eat
他们吃了 **Tāmen chī le** (tah-men CH luh)	They ate

咕噜肉 **gūlū ròu** (goo-loo-roe)	sweet and sour pork
他们吃了咕噜肉。 **Tāmen chī le gūlū ròu.** (tah-men CH luh goo-loo-roe)	They ate sweet and sour pork.
我们 **wǒmen** (wor-men)	we
我们没吃咕噜肉。我们吃了 披萨。 **Wǒmen méi chī gūlū ròu. Wǒmen chī le pīsà.** (wor-men may CH goo-loo-roe. Wor-men CH luh pee-sa)	We didn't eat sweet and sour pork. We ate pizza.
买 **mǎi** (my)	buy
我们买了咖啡。 **Wǒmen mǎi le kāfēi.** (wor-men my luh kah-fay)	We bought coffee.
我们买了咖啡。他们买了披 萨。 **Wǒmen mǎi le kāfēi. Tāmen mǎi le pīsà.** (wor-men my luh kah-fay. Tah-men my luh pee-sa)	We bought coffee. They bought pizza.
去 **qù** (chü)	go / go to / to go to
我们去 **Wǒmen qù** (wor-men chü)	We go / We go to
我们去了 **Wǒmen qù le** (wor-men chü luh)	We went / We went to

上海 **Shànghǎi** (SHanghai)	Shanghai
北京 **Běijīng** (bay-jing)	Beijing
我们去了上海，但是他们去了北京。 **Wǒmen qù le Shànghǎi, dànshì tāmen qù le Běijīng.** (wor-men chü luh SHanghai dan-SHi tah-men chü luh bay-jing)	We went to Shanghai but they went to Beijing.
打 **dǎ** (dah)	hit
麻将 **májiàng** (mah-jang)	mahjong
她打麻将。 **Tā dǎ májiàng.** (tah dah mah-jang)	She plays mahjong – literally "She hits mahjong".
她打了麻将。 **Tā dǎ le májiàng.** (tah dah luh mah-jang)	She played mahjong.
她打了麻将吗？ **Tā dǎ le májiàng ma?** (tah dah luh mah-jang mah)	Did she play mahjong?
我的 **wǒde** (wor-duh)	my
我的钱 **wǒde qián** (wor-duh chee-en)	my money
哪里？ **Nǎlǐ?** (nah-lee)	Where?

我的钱去了哪里？ **Wǒde qián qù le nǎlǐ?** (wor-duh chee-en chü luh nah-lee)	Where did my money go?
你的 **nǐde** (nee-duh)	your
你的钱去了哪里？ **Nǐde qián qù le nǎlǐ?** (nee-duh chee-en chü luh nah-lee)	Where did your money go?
我们去了上海，打了麻将。 **Wǒmen qù le Shànghǎi, dǎ le májiàng.** (wor-men chü luh SHanghai, dah luh mah-jang)	We went to Shanghai and played mahjong.
学了 **xué le** (shüwair luh)	learned / studied
功夫 **gōng fū** (gong foo)	kung fu
我们学了功夫。 **Wǒmen xué le gōng fū.** (wor-men shüwair luh gong foo)	We learned kung fu.
太极 **tàijí** (ty-jee)	tai chi
我们学了功夫，但是他们学了太极。 **Wǒmen xué le gōng fū, dànshì tāmen xué le tàijí.** (wor-men shüwair luh gong foo dan-SHi tah-men shüwair luh ty-jee)	We learned kung fu but they learned tai chi.
你们 **nǐmen** (nee-men)	you (MTOP)

你们学了太极吗？ **Nǐmen xué le tàijí ma?** (nee-men shüwair luh ty-jee mah)	Did you learn tai chi? (MTOP)
中文 **Zhōngwén** (ZHong-wen)	Chinese
你们学了中文吗？ **Nǐmen xué le Zhōngwén ma?** (nee-men shüwair luh ZHong-wen mah)	Did you learn Chinese? (MTOP)
英文 **Yīngwén** (ying-wen)	English
你们学了英文吗？ **Nǐmen xué le Yīngwén ma?** (nee-men shüwair luh ying-wen mah)	Did you learn English? (MTOP)

Now, time to do it the other way around!

you	你 **nǐ** (nee)
want	要 **yào** (yow)
You want	你要 **Nǐ yào** (nee yow)
fried	炒 **chǎo** (CHow)
noodles	面 **miàn** (mee-en)

fried noodles / chow mein	炒面 **chǎo miàn** (CHow mee-en)
You want fried noodles / chow mein.	你要炒面。 **Nǐ yào chǎo miàn.** (nee yow CHow mee-en)
tofu	豆腐 **dòufu** (doe-foo)
You want tofu.	你要豆腐。 **Nǐ yào dòufu.** (nee yow doe-foo)
spoken question mark	吗？ **ma?** (mah)
Do you want tofu?	你要豆腐吗？ **Nǐ yào dòufu ma?** (nee yow doe-foo mah)
and	和 **hé** (her)
Do you want fried noodles and tofu?	你要炒面和豆腐吗？ **Nǐ yào chǎo miàn hé dòufu ma?** (nee yow CHow mee-en her doe-foo mah)
rice	饭 **fàn** (fan)
fried rice	炒饭 **chǎo fàn** (CHow fan)
Do you want fried rice and tofu?	你要炒饭和豆腐吗？ **Nǐ yào chǎo fàn hé dòufu ma?** (nee yow CHow fan her doe-foo mah)
not	不 **bù** (boo)

Don't you want fried rice and tofu?	你不要炒饭和豆腐吗？ **Nǐ bù yào chǎo fàn hé dòufu ma?** *(nee boo yow CHow fan her doe-foo mah)*
I	我 **wǒ** *(wor)*
I want	我要 **Wǒ yào** *(wor yow)*
I want fried rice and tofu.	我要炒饭和豆腐。 **Wǒ yào chǎo fàn hé dòufu.** *(wor yow CHow fan her doe-foo)*
I don't want	我不要 **Wǒ bù yào** *(wor boo yow)*
I don't want fried rice and tofu.	我不要炒饭和豆腐。 **Wǒ bù yào chǎo fàn hé dòufu.** *(wor boo yow CHow fan her doe-foo)*
I know.	我知道。 **Wǒ zhīdào.** *(wor ZHi-dow)*
I know you want fried noodles.	我知道你要炒面。 **Wǒ zhīdào nǐ yào chǎo miàn.** *(wor ZHi-dow nee yow CHow mee-en)*
I don't know.	我不知道。 **Wǒ bù zhīdào.** *(wor boo ZHi-dow)*
maybe	也许 **yěxǔ** *(ye-shü)*
I don't know. Maybe.	我不知道。也许。 **Wǒ bù zhīdào. Yěxǔ.** *(wor boo ZHi-dow. ye-shü)*

a little / a bit of	一点 **yīdiǎn** (ee-dee-en)
coffee	咖啡 **kāfēi** (kah-fay)
She wants	她要 **Tā yào** (tah yow)
She wants a little coffee.	她要一点咖啡。 **Tā yào yīdiǎn kāfēi.** (tah yow ee-dee-en kah-fay)
Does she want a little coffee?	她要一点咖啡吗？ **Tā yào yīdiǎn kāfēi ma?** (tah yow ee-dee-en kah-fay mah)
He wants	他要 **Tā yào** (tah yow)
tea	茶 **chá** (CHah)
He wants a little tea.	他要一点茶。 **Tā yào yīdiǎn chá.** (tah yow ee-dee-en CHah)
Does he want a little tea?	他要一点茶吗？ **Tā yào yīdiǎn chá ma?** (tah yow ee-dee-en CHah mah)
Does he want a bit of fried rice?	他要一点炒饭吗？ **Tā yào yīdiǎn chǎo fàn ma?** (tah yow ee-dee-en CHow fan mah)
a bit more / a little more	多一点 **duō yīdiǎn** (dwor ee-dee-en)
Does he want a bit more fried rice?	他要多一点炒饭吗？ **Tā yào duō yīdiǎn chǎo fàn ma?** (tah yow dwor ee-dee-en CHow fan mah)

cola / coke	可乐 **kělè** (ker-ler)
Does he want a little more coke?	他要多一点可乐吗？ **Tā yào duō yīdiǎn kělè ma?** (tah yow dwor ee-dee-en ker-ler mah)
snack	点心 **diǎnxīn** (dee-en-syin)
She wants a snack.	她要点心。 **Tā yào diǎnxīn.** (tah yow dee-en-syin)
Cantonese-style	广式 **guǎng shì** (gwung SHi)
dim sum / Cantonese-style snack	广式点心 **guǎng shì diǎnxīn** (gwung SHi dee-en-syin)
She wants dim sum.	她要广式点心。 **Tā yào guǎng shì diǎnxīn.** (tah yow gwung SHi dee-en-syin)
dot / point / order	点 **diǎn** (dee-en)
I order	我点 **Wǒ diǎn** (wor dee-en)
I ordered	我点了 **Wǒ diǎn le** (wor dee-en luh)
I ordered tea, coffee, and dim sum.	我点了茶、咖啡和广式点心。 **Wǒ diǎn le chá, kāfēi hé guǎng shì diǎnxīn.** (wor dee-en luh CHah, kah-fay her gwung SHi dee-en-syin)

money	钱 **qián** (chee-en)
pay (literally "pay money")	付钱 **fù qián** (foo chee-en)
You pay	你付钱 **Nǐ fù qián** (nee foo chee-en)
You paid	你付了钱 **Nǐ fù le qián** (nee foo luh chee-en)
Did you pay?	你付了钱吗？ **Nǐ fù le qián ma?** (nee foo luh chee-en mah)
didn't	没 **méi** (may)
He didn't pay	他没付钱 **Tā méi fù qián** (tah may foo chee-en)
but	但是 **dànshì** (dan-SHi)
He ordered tea, coffee, and dim sum but he didn't pay!	他点了茶、咖啡和广式点心，但是他没付钱！ **Tā diǎn le chá, kāfēi hé guǎng shì diǎnxīn, dànshì tā méi fù qián!** (tah dee-en luh CHah, kah-fay her gwung SHi dee-en-syin dan-SHi tah may foo chee-en)
they	他们 **tāmen** (tah-men)

pizza	披萨 **pīsà** (pee-sa)
They ordered pizza but they didn't pay!	他们点了披萨，但是他们没付钱！ **Tāmen diǎn le pīsà, dànshì tāmen méi fù qián!** (tah-men *dee-en* luh pee-sa dan-SHi tah-men may foo chee-en)
eat	吃 **chī** (CH)
They eat	他们吃 **Tāmen chī** (tah-men CH)
They ate	他们吃了 **Tāmen chī le** (tah-men CH luh)
sweet and sour pork	咕噜肉 **gūlū ròu** (goo-loo-roe)
They ate sweet and sour pork.	他们吃了咕噜肉。 **Tāmen chī le gūlū ròu.** (tah-men CH luh goo-loo-roe)
we	我们 **wǒmen** (wor-men)
We didn't eat sweet and sour pork. We ate pizza.	我们没吃咕噜肉。我们吃了披萨。 **Wǒmen méi chī gūlū ròu. Wǒmen chī le pīsà.** (wor-men may CH goo-loo-roe. Wor-men CH luh pee-sa)
buy	买 **mǎi** (my)

We bought coffee.	我们买了咖啡。 **Wǒmen mǎi le kāfēi.** (wor-men my luh kah-fay)
We bought coffee. They bought pizza.	我们买了咖啡。他们买了披萨。 **Wǒmen mǎi le kāfēi. Tāmen mǎi le pīsà.** (wor-men my luh kah-fay. Tah-men my luh pee-sa)
go / go to / to go to	去 **qù** (chü)
We go / We go to	我们去 **Wǒmen qù** (wor-men chü)
We went / We went to	我们去了 **Wǒmen qù le** (wor-men chü luh)
Shanghai	上海 **Shànghǎi** (SHanghai)
Beijing	北京 **Běijīng** (bay-jing)
We went to Shanghai but they went to Beijing.	我们去了上海，但是他们去了北京。 **Wǒmen qù le Shànghǎi, dànshì tāmen qù le Běijīng.** (wor-men chü luh SHanghai dan-SHi tah-men chü luh bay-jing)
hit	打 **dǎ** (dah)
mahjong	麻将 **májiàng** (mah-jang)

She plays mahjong – literally "She hits mahjong".	她打麻将。 **Tā dǎ májiàng.** (tah dah mah-jang)
She played mahjong.	她打了麻将。 **Tā dǎ le májiàng.** (tah dah luh mah-jang)
Did she play mahjong?	她打了麻将吗？ **Tā dǎ le májiàng ma?** (tah dah luh mah-jang mah)
my	我的 **wǒde** (wor-duh)
my money	我的钱 **wǒde qián** (wor-duh chee-en)
Where?	哪里？ **Nǎlǐ?** (nah-lee)
Where did my money go?	我的钱去了哪里？ **Wǒde qián qù le nǎlǐ?** (wor-duh chee-en chü luh nah-lee)
your	你的 **nǐde** (nee-duh)
Where did your money go?	你的钱去了哪里？ **Nǐde qián qù le nǎlǐ?** (nee-duh chee-en chü luh nah-lee)
We went to Shanghai and played mahjong.	我们去了上海，打了麻将。 **Wǒmen qù le Shànghǎi, dǎ le májiàng.** (wor-men chü luh SHanghai, dah luh mah-jang)
learned / studied	学了 **xué le** (shüwair luh)

kung fu	功夫 **gōng fū** (gong foo)
We learned kung fu.	我们学了功夫。 **Wǒmen xué le gōng fū.** (wor-men shüwair luh gong foo)
tai chi	太极 **tàijí** (ty-jee)
We learned kung fu but they learned tai chi.	我们学了功夫，但是他们学了太极。 **Wǒmen xué le gōng fū, dànshì tāmen xué le tàijí.** (wor-men shüwair luh gong foo dan-SHi tah-men shüwair luh ty-jee)
you (MTOP)	你们 **nǐmen** (nee-men)
Did you learn tai chi? (MTOP)	你们学了太极吗？ **Nǐmen xué le tàijí ma?** (nee-men shüwair luh ty-jee mah)
Chinese	中文 **Zhōngwén** (ZHong-wen)
Did you learn Chinese? (MTOP)	你们学了中文吗？ **Nǐmen xué le Zhōngwén ma?** (nee-men shüwair luh ZHong-wen mah)
English	英文 **Yīngwén** (ying-wen)
Did you learn English? (MTOP)	你们学了英文吗？ **Nǐmen xué le Yīngwén ma?** (nee-men shüwair luh ying-wen mah)

Well, that's it, you're done with Chapter 3! Take a break!

Use your "hidden moments"

A famous American linguist, Barry Farber, learned a great part of the languages he spoke during the "hidden moments" he found in everyday life. Such hidden moments might include the time he would spend waiting for a train to arrive or time spent waiting for the kids to come out of school or for the traffic to get moving in the morning. These hidden moments would otherwise have been useless and unimportant in his daily life but, for someone learning a language, they can be some of the most useful minutes of the day.

Breaking up your studies into lots of little bits like this can also be useful as a way to help stop them from feeling like a great effort or from becoming impractical when your life gets especially hectic.

So, keep this book in your pocket whenever you go out and then make use of such "hidden moments" whenever they come along!

Yuanmingyuan, the Old Summer Palace

CHAPTER 4 (1)

I'm planning to go to China in May. (part 1)

You tell people you're going on a trip far away and the first thing they want is details. Where? When? Why?

Don't they realise there's a reason why you're going away without them?

Now, remind me, what is "learned"?

学了
xué le
(shüwair luh)

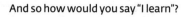

So what is "learn"?

学
xué
(shüwair)

And so how would you say "I learn"?

我学
wǒ xué
(wor shüwair)

What is "Chinese" – literally "middle language"?

中文
Zhōngwén
(ZHong-wen)

And so how would you say "I learn Chinese"?

我学中文。
Wǒ xué Zhōngwén.
(wor shüwair ZHong-wen)

How about "He learns Chinese"?

他学中文。
Tā xué Zhōngwén.
(tah shüwair ZHong-wen)

And "She learns Chinese"?

她学中文。
Tā xué Zhōngwén.
(tah shüwair ZHong-wen)

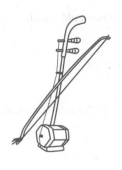

And how would you say "She learned Chinese"?

她学了中文。
Tā xué le Zhōngwén.
(tah shüwair luh ZHong-wen)

What is "English" – literally "brave language"?

英文
Yīngwén
(ying-wen)

And so how would you say "She learned English"?

她学了英文。
Tā xué le Yīngwén.
(tah shüwair luh ying-wen)

And "Did she learn English?"

她学了英文吗？
Tā xué le Yīngwén ma?
(tah shüwair luh ying-wen mah)

What is "kung fu"?

功夫
gōng fū
(gong foo)

And so how would you say "She learned kung fu"?

她学了功夫。
Tā xué le gōng fū.
(tah shüwair luh gong-foo)

What about "Did she learn kung fu?"

她学了功夫吗？
Tā xué le gōng fū ma?
(tah shüwair luh gong-foo mah)

What is "tai chi"?

太极
tàijí
(ty-jee)

And so how would you say "Did she learn tai chi?"

她学了太极吗？
Tā xué le tàijí ma?
(tah shüwair luh ty-jee mah)

What is "go"?

去
qù
(chü)

And how would you say "she goes"?

她去
tā qù
(tah chü)

And "she went"?

她去了
tā qù le
(tah chü luh)

And that means both "she went" and "she went to".

So how would you say "She went to Shanghai"?

她去了上海。
Tā qù le Shànghǎi.
(tah chü luh SHanghai)

How about "She went to Beijing"?

她去了北京。
Tā qù le Běijīng.
(tah chü luh bay-jing)

And again what was "Chinese" – literally "middle language"?

中文
Zhōngwén
(ZHong-wen)

So if "Zhōngwén" means "middle language", what do you think the Chinese word for "middle" is?

中
zhōng
(ZHong)

"China" in Chinese is:

中国
Zhōngguó
(ZHong-gwor)

And this literally means "middle kingdom" or "middle country".

So how would you say "She went to China"?

她去了中国。
Tā qù le Zhōngguó.
(tah chü luh ZHong-gwor)

And "They went to China"?

他们去了中国。
Tāmen qù le Zhōngguó.
(tah-men chü luh ZHong-gwor)

How about "Did they go to China?"

他们去了中国吗？
Tāmen qù le Zhōngguó ma?
(tah-men chü luh ZHong-gwor mah)

"I plan to" or "I'm planning to" is:

我打算
wǒ dǎsuàn
(wor dah-swann[18])

Now again, what is "go"?

去
qù
(chü)

And actually that can mean "go", "go to" and "to go to" – Chinese is much simpler than English in this regard. One word in Chinese often covers many in English!

So, if "I plan" or "I'm planning" is:

我打算
wǒ dǎsuàn
(wor dah-swann)

How would you say "I'm planning to go"?

我打算去
wǒ dǎsuàn qù
(wor dah-swann chü)

And again what is "China"?

中国
Zhōngguó
(ZHong-gwor)

---

18 The part of the word I've written as "swann" in the pronunciation guidance should be pronounced to rhyme with "can" or "fan". I have avoided spelling the pronunciation guidance as "swan" out of fear that you might then pronounce it like the name of the bird! So, pronounce "swann" with the "an" pronounced like the "an" in "can" and you'll be understood!

And so how would you say "I'm planning to go to China"?

我打算去中国。
Wǒ dǎsuàn qù Zhōngguó.
(wor dah-swann chü ZHong-gwor)

And "I'm planning to go to Shanghai"?

我打算去上海。
Wǒ dǎsuàn qù Shànghǎi.
(wor dah-swann chü SHanghai)

And how about "I'm planning to go to Beijing"?

我打算去北京。
Wǒ dǎsuàn qù Běijīng.
(wor dah-swann chü bay-jing)

The months of the year in Chinese are surprisingly easy to learn; this is because they are simply numbers added to the word for moon. I'll show you what I mean.

Again, what is "a little" or "a bit of"?

一点
yīdiǎn
(ee-dee-en)

And that actually literally means "one point" or "one dot". So, as that's the case, what is "one" in Chinese?

一
yī
(ee)

"Month" in Chinese is:

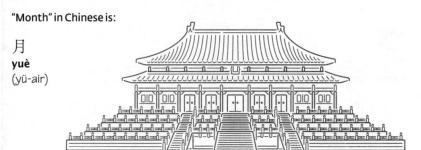

月
yuè
(yü-air)

So how would you literally say "one month"?

一月
yī yuè
(*ee* yü-air)

And that means "January" in Chinese, which is fairly logical really: number one month = January.

So, number one month in Chinese is January, number two month is February, number three month is March, and so on.

This means of course that, once you know the numbers one to twelve in Chinese, then you also know the names of the months.

So, once again, what is "month"?

月
yuè
(yü-air)

And what is "one"?

一
yī
(*ee*)

And so what is "January"?

一月
yī yuè
(*ee* yü-air)

"Five" is:

五
wǔ
(*woo*)

So how would you say "May" – literally "5 month"?

五月
wǔ yuè
(*woo* yü-air)

To say "*in* May", you will also say exactly the same thing, as there's no difference in Chinese between saying "May" and "in May". So how would you say "in May"?

五月
wǔ yuè
(woo yü-air)

Now again, what is "I plan to" or "I'm planning to"?

我打算
wǒ dǎsuàn
(wor dah-swann)

And what is "I'm planning to go"?

我打算去
wǒ dǎsuàn qù
(wor dah-swann chü)

And "I'm planning to go to China"?

我打算去中国。
Wǒ dǎsuàn qù Zhōngguó.
(wor dah-swann chü ZHong-gwor)

And once again if "five" is "**wǔ**" and "month" is "**yuè**", how would you say "May"?

五月
wǔ yuè
(woo yü-air)

And how would you say "in May"?

五月
wǔ yuè
(woo yü-air)

Now, if you want to say "I'm planning to go to China in May", you will literally say "I'm planning in May to go to China." Let's say that now, but we'll do this in steps, building it up, part by part.

Again, what is "I'm planning"?

我打算
wǒ dǎsuàn
(wor dah-swann)

And "I'm planning in May"?

我打算五月
wǒ dǎsuàn wǔ yuè
(wor dah-swann woo yü-air)

And "I'm planning in May to go"?

我打算五月去
wǒ dǎsuàn wǔ yuè qù
(wor dah-swann woo yü-air chü)

And now say "I'm planning to go to China in May." / "I'm planning in May to go to China."

我打算五月去中国。
Wǒ dǎsuàn wǔ yuè qù Zhōngguó.
(wor dah-swann woo yü-air chü ZHong-gwor)

And how about "I'm planning to go to Shanghai in May"?

我打算五月去上海。
Wǒ dǎsuàn wǔ yuè qù Shànghǎi.
(wor dah-swann woo yü-air chü SHanghai)

Now, if someone told you that they were planning to go to China in May, you might well want to ask "Oh, whereabouts in China?" And this is very easy to say in Chinese, particularly for you as you actually already know all the words you'll need in order to say it!

Again, what is "China"?

中国
Zhōngguó
(ZHong-gwor)

And do you remember how to say "where"?

哪里
nǎlǐ
(nah-lee)

If you want to say "Whereabouts in China?" you simply need to say "China where?" How would you say that?

中国哪里？
Zhōngguó nǎlǐ?
(ZHong-gwor nah-lee)

"Oh" in Chinese is more or less the same as it is in English:

喔
Ō
(oh)

So how would you say "Oh, whereabouts in China?" – literally "Oh, China where?"

喔，中国哪里？
Ō, Zhōngguó nǎlǐ?
(oh ZHong-gwor nah-lee)

What is "Chinese" – literally "middle language"?

中文
Zhōngwén
(ZHong-wen)

And again, what is "China" – literally "middle kingdom"?

中国
Zhōngguó
(ZHong-gwor)

And what is "English" – literally "brave language"?

英文
Yīngwén
(ying-wen)

Can you guess what "Britain" will be in Chinese – literally "brave kingdom"?

英国
Yīngguó
(ying-gwor)

What is "I'm planning to"?

我打算
wǒ dǎsuàn
(wor dah-swann)

And so how would you say "I'm planning to go to Britain"?

我打算去英国。
Wǒ dǎsuàn qù Yīngguó.
(wor dah-swann chü ying-gwor)

And again what is "May" / "in May"?

五月
wǔ yuè
(woo yü-air)

And so how would you say "I'm planning to go to Britain in May"?

我打算五月去英国。
Wǒ dǎsuàn wǔ yuè qù Yīngguó.
(wor dah-swann woo yü-air chü ying-gwor)

And how about "You're planning to go to Britain in May"?

你打算五月去英国。
Nǐ dǎsuàn wǔ yuè qù Yīngguó.
(nee dah-swann woo yü-air chü ying-gwor)

Turn that into a question by adding "ma" onto the end of it and ask "Are you planning to go to Britain in May?"

你打算五月去英国吗？
Nǐ dǎsuàn wǔ yuè qù Yīngguó ma?
(nee dah-swann woo yü-air chü ying-gwor mah)

And again, how would you say "Are you planning to go to China in May?"

你打算五月去中国吗？
Nǐ dǎsuàn wǔ yuè qù Zhōngguó ma?
(nee dah-swann woo yü-air chü ZHong-gwor mah)

Now once more what was "Where?"

哪里？
Nǎlǐ?
(nah-lee)

And so how would you say "Whereabouts in China?" – literally "China where?"

中国哪里？
Zhōngguó nǎlǐ?
(ZHong-gwor nah-lee)

If someone asks you a question like that, you could answer by saying "I don't know". How would you say that?

我不知道。
Wǒ bù zhīdào.
(wor boo ZHi-dow)

"Yet" in Chinese is:

还
hái
(hy[19])

If you want to say "I don't know yet", you'll literally say "I yet not know", how would you say that?

我还不知道。
Wǒ hái bù zhīdào.
(wor hy boo ZHi-dow)

What about "He doesn't know yet"?

他还不知道。
Tā hái bù zhīdào.
(tah hy boo ZHi-dow)

(double happiness)

And "They don't know yet"?

他们还不知道。
Tāmen hái bù zhīdào.
(tah-men hy *boo* ZHi-dow)

How about "You don't know yet"?

你还不知道。
Nǐ hái bù zhīdào.
(nee hy *boo* ZHi-dow)

What is "you" when you're talking to more than one person?

你们
nǐmen
(nee-men)

And so how would you say "You don't know yet"? (MTOP)

你们还不知道。
Nǐmen hái bù zhīdào.
(nee-men hy *boo* ZHi-dow)

And "Don't you know yet?" (MTOP)

你们还不知道吗？
Nǐmen hái bù zhīdào ma?
(nee-men hy *boo* ZHi-dow mah)

What is "maybe"?

也许
yěxǔ
(ye-shü)

If you were asked where exactly you were going in China, how would you answer "maybe Beijing"?

也许北京。
Yěxǔ Běijīng.
(ye-shü bay-jing)

How about "maybe Shanghai"?

也许上海。
Yěxǔ Shànghǎi.
(ye-shü SHanghai)

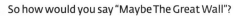

"The Great Wall" in Chinese is:

长城
Chángchéng
(CHang-CHerng)

So how would you say "Maybe The Great Wall"?

也许长城。
Yěxǔ Chángchéng.
(ye-shü CHang-CHerng)

Again, what is "I'm planning to"?

我打算
wǒ dǎsuàn
(wor dah-swann)

And "I'm planning to go" / "I'm planning to go to"?

我打算去
wǒ dǎsuàn qù
(wor dah-swann chü)

And, as I said just a moment ago, "The Great Wall" in Chinese is:

长城
Chángchéng
(CHang-CHerng)

So how would you say "I'm planning to go to The Great Wall"?

我打算去长城。
Wǒ dǎsuàn qù Chángchéng.
(wor dah-swann chü CHang-CHerng)

What is "in May"?

五月
wǔ yuè
(woo yü-air)

And so how would you say "I'm planning to go to The Great Wall in May" / "I'm planning in May to go to The Great Wall"?

我打算五月去长城。
Wǒ dǎsuàn wǔ yuè qù Chángchéng.
(wor dah-swann woo yü-air chü CHang-CHerng)

And how would you say "I'm planning to go to China in May"?

我打算五月去中国。
Wǒ dǎsuàn wǔ yuè qù Zhōngguó.
(wor dah-swann woo yü-air chü ZHong-gwor)

How would someone reply to that saying "Oh, whereabouts in China?"

喔，中国哪里？
Ō, Zhōngguó nǎlǐ?
(oh ZHong-gwor nah-lee)

And how would you answer that question saying "I don't know"?

我不知道。
Wǒ bù zhīdào.
(wor boo ZHi-dow)

What is "yet"?

还
hái
(hy)

And so how would you answer saying "I don't know yet"?

我还不知道。
Wǒ hái bù zhīdào.
(wor hy boo ZHi-dow)

How about "I don't know yet, maybe Beijing"?

我还不知道，也许北京。
Wǒ hái bù zhīdào, yěxǔ Běijīng.
(wor hy boo ZHi-dow ye-shü bay-jing)

Now again, what was "The Great Wall"?

长城
Chángchéng
(CHang-CHerng)

And so how would you say "I don't know yet, maybe The Great Wall"?

我还不知道，也许长城。
Wǒ hái bù zhīdào, yěxǔ Chángchéng.
(wor hy boo ZHi-dow ye-shü CHang-CHerng)

And how about "I don't know yet. Maybe Shanghai, Beijing, The Great Wall"?

我还不知道，也许上海、北京、长城。
Wǒ hái bù zhīdào, yěxǔ Shànghǎi, Běijīng, Chángchéng.
(wor hy boo ZHi-dow ye-shü SHanghai bay-jing CHang-CHerng)

Excellent. Well, let's try putting all of this together so that you can go through the entire dialogue from the beginning of the chapter in one go. Work your way through it, nice and slow:

I'm planning to go to China in May.

我打算五月去中国。
Wǒ dǎsuàn wǔ yuè qù Zhōngguó.
(wor dah-swann woo yü-air chü ZHong-gwor)

Oh, whereabouts in China?

喔，中国哪里？
Ō, Zhōngguó nǎlǐ?
(oh ZHong-gwor nah-lee)

I don't know yet. Maybe Shanghai, Beijing, The Great Wall.

我还不知道，也许上海、北京、长城。

Wǒ hái bù zhīdào, yěxǔ Shànghǎi, Běijīng, Chángchéng.

(wor hy boo ZHi-dow ye-shü SHanghai bay-jing CHang-CHerng)

Wow, that was an extremely complex dialogue with a lot of different ideas and phrases in it to be juggled. If you felt unclear regarding how to construct any of the different parts it was made up of, do feel free to go back to the beginning of the chapter. And you should feel welcome to do this at any point when you feel constructing a sentence is becoming a struggle. There is no rush. You should always only work at a pace that feels suitable for you. And, when you do get to the point where you can get through this entire dialogue without making mistakes, it can still be worth practising it a few times so as to help build your confidence and fluency in using what you've learned.

If you've done all that then prepare to get excited as we are now going to expand and develop this dialogue even further as we venture into the next chapter!

CHAPTER 4 (2)

I'm planning to go to China in May. (part 2)

> I'm planning to go to China in May.
> Oh, whereabouts in China?
> I don't know yet, Shanghai, Beijing, maybe
> The Great Wall.
> Have you been before?
> Erm, I've been to Chinatown.
> Mmh, that doesn't count.

As you can see, I have extended the dialogue from the previous chapter. You are now going to learn how to complete this conversation, building on what you've learned already, expanding your range of Chinese expressions as we go.

First of all, remind me, how would you say "I'm planning to"?

我打算
wǒ dǎsuàn
(wor dah-swann)

And how would you say "I'm planning to go to China"?

我打算去中国。
Wǒ dǎsuàn qù Zhōngguó.
(wor dah-swann chü ZHong-gwor)

How about "I'm planning to go to China in May"?

我打算五月去中国。
Wǒ dǎsuàn wǔ yuè qù Zhōngguó.
(wor dah-swann woo yü-air chü ZHong-gwor)

And how would you say "Oh, whereabouts in China?"

喔，中国哪里？
Ō, Zhōngguó nǎlǐ?
(oh ZHong-gwor nah-lee)

What is "I don't know"?

我不知道。
Wǒ bù zhīdào.
(wor boo ZHi-dow)

And "I don't know yet"?

我还不知道。
Wǒ hái bù zhīdào.
(wor hy boo ZHi-dow)

What is "maybe"?

也许
yěxǔ
(ye-shü)

And what is "The Great Wall"?

长城
Chángchéng
(CHang-CHerng)

And so how would you say "I don't know yet. Maybe Shanghai, Beijing, The Great Wall"?

我还不知道，也许上海、北京、长城。
Wǒ hái bù zhīdào, yěxǔ Shànghǎi, Běijīng, Chángchéng.
(wor hy boo ZHi-dow ye-shü SHanghai bay-jing CHang-CHerng)

What is "I eat"?

我吃
wǒ chī
(wor CH)

And what is "sweet and sour pork"?

咕噜肉
gūlū ròu
(goo-loo-roe)

So how would you say "I eat sweet and sour pork"?

我吃咕噜肉。
Wǒ chī gūlū ròu.
(wor CH goo-loo-roe)

How about "I ate sweet and sour pork"?

我吃了咕噜肉。
Wǒ chī le gūlū ròu.
(wor CH luh goo-loo-roe)

And what about "I ate dim sum"?

我吃了广式点心。
Wǒ chī le guǎng shì diǎnxīn.
(wor CH luh gwung SHi dee-en-syin)

And "I ate fried noodles"?

我吃了炒面。
Wǒ chī le chǎo miàn.
(wor CH luh CHow mee-en)

What is "I go"?

我去
wǒ qù
(wor chü)

And what is "I went"?

我去了
wǒ qù le
(wor chü luh)

So how would you say "I went to The Great Wall"?

我去了长城。
Wǒ qù le Chángchéng.
(wor chü luh CHang-CHerng)

What about "I went to China"?

我去了中国。
Wǒ qù le Zhōngguó.
(wor chü luh ZHong-gwor)

Now, in English, there is a difference between "I went to" and "I have gone to" and there is also a difference between them in Chinese.

Once more, what is "I go"?

我去
wǒ qù
(wor chü)

Now, whenever you've wanted to turn "I go" into "I went" you've simply added "**le**" onto the end of "I go".

If, on the other hand, you want to say "I've gone" rather than "I went", you'll simply add a different word onto the end of "I go".

Again, what is "I go"?

我去
wǒ qù
(wor chü)

I now want you add "**guò**" onto the end of this. Doing so, what do you end up with?

我去过
wǒ qù guò
(wor chü gwor[20])

And this means "I have gone".

So again, what is "I go"?

我去
wǒ qù
(wor chü)

---

20 By the way, in case you're wondering whether this is the same "**guò**" as you find inside the Chinese word for "China" (**Zhōngguó**) it isn't. Just as in English, sometimes two different words just happen to sound similar or the same.

And what is "I went"?

我去了
wǒ qù le
(wor chü luh)

And what is "I have gone"?

我去过
wǒ qù guò
(wor chü gwor)

Now that you know how to say "I have gone", you might be wondering, "Well, what's the difference exactly between "I went' and 'I've gone', what's the difference between using '**le**' and '**guò**'?"

Well, we have used "**le**" simply to say that something happened at some point earlier in time. For instance "I ordered a pizza", "I went to China", "I ate sweet and sour pork". So we've used "**le**" for simply talking about something that happened in the past.

When we use "**guò**", however, it's a bit different. Using "**guò**" is for talking about an *experience* you've had before. In fact, in English, we'll often add the word "before" to such sentences. I'll show you what I mean.

Again, what is "I go"?

我去
wǒ qù
(wor chü)

And what is "I have gone"? Or, if you prefer to think of it that way, "I have gone *before*". How would you say that?

我去过
wǒ qù guò
(wor chü gwor)

And so how would you say "I have gone to China" / "I have gone to China before"?

我去过中国。
Wǒ qù guò Zhōngguó.
(wor chü gwor ZHong-gwor)

So, as you can see, when you want to explain that you've had the experience of doing something before, in this case you've gone to China before, in Chinese you'll use "**guò**" to indicate that. Let's try some more examples of this.

What is "I eat"?

我吃
wǒ chī
(wor CH)

And what is "I ate"?

我吃了
wǒ chī le
(wor CH luh)

And so how do you think you would you say "I have eaten" or "I have eaten *before*"?

我吃过
wǒ chī guò
(wor CH gwor)

And so how would you say "I've eaten sweet and sour pork before"?

我吃过咕噜肉。
Wǒ chī guò gūlū ròu.
(wor CH gwor goo-loo-roe)

How about "I've eaten dim sum before"?

我吃过广式点心。
Wǒ chī guò guǎng shì diǎnxīn.
(wor CH gwor gwung SHi dee-en-syin)

And "I've eaten fried rice before"?

我吃过炒饭。
Wǒ chī guò chǎo fàn.
(wor CH gwor CHow fan)

What about "You've eaten fried rice before"?

你吃过炒饭。
Nǐ chī guò chǎo fàn.
(*nee* CH *gwor* CHow *fan*)

And how would you ask "Have you eaten fried rice before?" / "You've eaten fried rice before ma?"

你吃过炒饭吗？
Nǐ chī guò chǎo fàn ma?
(*nee* CH *gwor* CHow *fan mah*)

How about "Have you eaten sweet and sour pork before?"

你吃过咕噜肉吗？
Nǐ chī guò gūlū ròu ma?
(*nee* CH *gwor goo-loo-roe mah*)

So, as you can see, "**guò**" is all about talking about things you've done before, for telling people when you've had the experience of doing something before. Just as in English, there is a clear difference between saying "I ate sweet and sour pork yesterday" and saying "Yeah, I've eaten sweet and sour pork before. Who hasn't?" In Chinese the first sentence would use "**le**" and the second would use "**guò**".

Now again, how would you say "You have gone before"?

你去过。
Nǐ qù guò
(*nee chü gwor*)

And how would you say "You have gone to China before"?

你去过中国。
Nǐ qù guò Zhōngguó.
(*nee chü gwor* ZHong-*gwor*)

By the way, it's worth mentioning that, in English, rather than saying "I've gone before" we often instead say "I've been before". So, for example, although it is possible in English to say "Have you gone to China before?" it is perhaps even more typical to say "Have you been to China before?" In Chinese, both are said in exactly the same way.

So how would you say "You've gone to China before"?

你去过中国。
Nǐ qù guò Zhōngguó.
(nee chü gwor ZHong-gwor)

And how would you say "You've been to China before"?

你去过中国。
Nǐ qù guò Zhōngguó.
(nee chü gwor ZHong-gwor)

So they're the same. I'll generally translate these sentences using "been to" from now on, as it's what we're more likely to use in English for such sentences.

So how would you ask "Have you been to China before?"

你去过中国吗？
Nǐ qù guò Zhōngguó ma?
(nee chü gwor ZHong-gwor mah)

And how about "Has she been to China before?"

她去过中国吗？
Tā qù guò Zhōngguó ma?
(tah chü gwor ZHong-gwor mah)

"Singapore" in Chinese is:

新加坡
Xīnjiāpō
(syin-jah-pwor)

So how would you say "Has she been to Singapore before?"

她去过新加坡吗？
Tā qù guò Xīnjiāpō ma?
(tah chü gwor syin-jah-pwor mah)

What about "Have you been to Singapore before?"

你去过新加坡吗？
Nǐ qù guò Xīnjiāpō ma?
(nee chü gwor syin-jah-pwor mah)

And "Have they been to Singapore before?"

他们去过新加坡吗？
Tāmen qù guò Xīnjiāpō ma?
(tah-men chü gwor syin-jah-pwor mah)

What is "buy"?

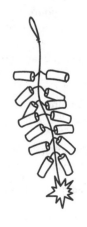

买
mǎi
(my)

And so how would you say "I buy"?

我买
wǒ mǎi
(wor my)

And "I bought"?

我买了
wǒ mǎi le
(wor my luh)

How about "I bought coffee"?

我买了咖啡。
Wǒ mǎi le kāfēi.
(wor my luh kah-fay)

And "I bought tea"?

我买了茶。
Wǒ mǎi le chá.
(wor my luh CHah)

"I bought coke"?

我买了可乐。
Wǒ mǎi le kělè.
(wor my luh ker-ler)

What about "I bought sweet and sour pork"?

我买了咕噜肉。
Wǒ mǎi le gūlū ròu.
(wor my luh goo-loo-roe)

And what would be "I have bought" / "I have bought before"?

我买过
wǒ mǎi guò
(wor my gwor)

And so how would you say "I've bought sweet and sour pork before"?

我买过咕噜肉。
Wǒ mǎi guò gūlū ròu.
(wor my gwor goo-loo-roe)

And "I've bought coke before"?

我买过可乐。
Wǒ mǎi guò kělè.
(wor my gwor ker-ler)

So, these examples should help make clear the difference between using "le" and "guò" to talk about the past. "Le" is really just for describing something that simply occurred whereas "guò" is how you make it clear that you've had the experience of doing something. "Guò" is what you would use, for example, if you felt someone was treating you as though you were totally incapable of doing a simple task, making you finally turn around and say – "Hey, I have bought coffee before you know. I wasn't born yesterday!" So, in short, it's simply there for talking about what you've had the experience of doing before.

What is "I order"?

我点
wǒ diǎn
(wor dee-en)

And "I ordered"?

我点了
wǒ diǎn le
(wor dee-en luh)

"I ordered tea"?

我点了茶。
Wǒ diǎn le chá.
(wor dee-en luh CHah)

And how would you say "I have ordered (before)"?

我点过
wǒ diǎn guò
(wor dee-en gwor)

And how would you say "I've ordered tea before"?

我点过茶。
Wǒ diǎn guò chá.
(wor dee-en gwor CHah)

Now again, what is "I've gone to (before)" / "I've been to (before)"?

我去过
wǒ qù guò
(wor chü gwor)

And what is "The Great Wall"?

长城
Chángchéng
(CHang-CHerng)

So how would you say "I've been to The Great Wall before"?

我去过长城。
Wǒ qù guò Chángchéng.
(wor chü gwor CHang-CHerng)

How about "You've been to The Great Wall before"?

你去过长城。
Nǐ qù guò Chángchéng.
(*nee chü gwor CHang-CHerng*)

And "Have you been to The Great Wall before?"

你去过长城吗？
Nǐ qù guò Chángchéng ma?
(*nee chü gwor CHang-CHerng mah*)

Now "**Chángchéng**" literally means "long wall" in Chinese. As that's the case, what is the word for "long" in Chinese?

长
cháng
(*chang*)

And what is the word for "wall"?

城
chéng
(*cherng*)

And what is "China"?

中国
Zhōngguó
(*ZHong-gwor*)

Time to create some words!
Word Building Practice Number 2

Remember how earlier we took the word "**yīdiǎn**" (a little / a bit of) and pulled it to bits to discover the number one (**yī**) inside it as well as the word for "dot", "point" and "order" (**diǎn**)?

Well, pulling words to bits and learning to build new ones is a crucial skill in Chinese, so let's practise doing it again.

This time, we'll take the word for "Great Wall". As you know, "**chángchéng**" literally means "long wall". So, just to remind me, which part means "long"?

Yes, good, it is indeed **cháng**.

And which part means "wall"?

Yes, again, excellent, it's **chéng**. I knew you'd get it right.

Well, let's take a look at that part that means "wall" (**chéng**). Actually, "**chéng**" could be translated not only as "wall", but also as "walled" and even as "walled-in". Anyway, let's use it to create a new bit of vocabulary.

What is China?

Yes, of course, it's **Zhōngguó**.

So let's put that together with "**chéng**" and say literally "China wall" / "China walled" / "China walled-in." Do that now. What is "China walled-in"?

Zhōngguóchéng

And that is actually how you say "Chinatown" in Chinese.

And it's logical in a way because Chinatown is in effect a bit of China within another country or city, a bit of China that's been walled-in by itself.

And this should show you just how amazing Chinese is! Words are made out of components and those components can be extracted and then used to create new vocabulary without any extra effort required to learn it. Awesome!

So again, what is "China"?

中国
Zhōngguó
(ZHong-gwor)

And what is "The Great Wall"?

长城
Chángchéng
(CHang-CHerng)

And what is "Chinatown" – literally "China walled-in"?

中国城
Zhōngguóchéng
(ZHong-gwor-cherng)

And so how would you say "I've been to Chinatown"?

我去过中国城。
Wǒ qù guò Zhōngguóchéng.
(wor chü gwor ZHong-gwor-cherng)

And "You've been to Chinatown"?

你去过中国城。
Nǐ qù guò Zhōngguóchéng.
(nee chü gwor ZHong-gwor-cherng)

And how would you ask "Have you been to Chinatown?"

你去过中国城吗？
Nǐ qù guò Zhōngguóchéng ma?
(nee chü gwor ZHong-gwor-cherng mah)

What is "I'm planning"?

我打算
wǒ dǎsuàn
(wor dah-swann)

And "I'm planning to go"?

我打算去
wǒ dǎsuàn qù
(wor dah-swann chü)

And how about "I'm planning to go to Chinatown"?

我打算去中国城。
Wǒ dǎsuàn qù Zhōngguóchéng.
(wor dah-swann chü ZHong-gwor-cherng)

What is "in May"?

五月
wǔ yuè
(woo yü-air)

So how would you say "I'm planning to go to Chinatown in May"?

我打算五月去中国城。
Wǒ dǎsuàn wǔ yuè qù Zhōngguóchéng.
(wor dah-swann woo yü-air chü ZHong-gwor-cherng)

What is the number "one"?

一
yī
(ee)

And so again, how would you say "January" – literally "one moon"?

一月
yī yuè
(ee yü-air)

And so how would you say "I'm planning to go to Chinatown in January"?

我打算一月去中国城。
Wǒ dǎsuàn yī yuè qù Zhōngguóchéng.
(wor dah-swann ee yü-air chü ZHong-gwor-cherng)

As I mentioned earlier, "Singapore" in Chinese is:

新加坡
Xīnjiāpō
(syin-jah-pwor)

So how would you say "I'm planning to go to Singapore in January"?

我打算一月去新加坡。
Wǒ dǎsuàn yī yuè qù Xīnjiāpō.
(wor dah-swann *ee* yü-air chü syin-jah-pwor)

What is "mahjong"?

麻将
májiàng
(mah-jang)

And what is "I play mahjong" – literally "I hit mahjong"?

我打麻将。
Wǒ dǎ májiàng.
(wor dah mah-jang)

And how about "I played mahjong"?

我打了麻将。
Wǒ dǎ le májiàng.
(wor dah luh mah-jang)

And "I've played mahjong before"?

我打过麻将。
Wǒ dǎ guò májiàng.
(wor dah gwor mah-jang)

And how would you say "You've played mahjong before"?

你打过麻将。
Nǐ dǎ guò májiàng.
(nee dah gwor mah-jang)

And what about "Have you played mahjong before?"

你打过麻将吗？

Nǐ dǎ guò májiàng ma?

(nee dah gwor mah-jang mah)

☀. Time to create some words!
Word Building Practice Number 3

"I'm planning to" / "**Wǒ dǎsuàn**" – you've used this phrase quite a lot. Let's pull it to bits and use it now to create some new vocabulary!

You're actually already familiar with the meaning of the first part of "**dǎsuàn**" – the "**dǎ**" – which literally means "hit" – you've been using it when talking about mahjong. However, you don't yet know what the second part of "**dǎsuàn**" – the "**suàn**" – means.

Well, this "**suàn**" part actually means "count". So, "I'm planning to" – **wǒ dǎsuàn** – literally means "I hit the count" in Chinese.

Sound weird?

Well, it sounded odd to me too when I first learned its meaning many moons ago but nowadays I like to think that the logic behind it is that, effectively, you're hitting the count you expected, so you can plan for what's going to happen. So, **dǎsuàn**: to plan, to hit the count.

Anyway, the precise logic behind **dǎsuàn** doesn't really matter that much, so long as you know that "**wǒ dǎsuàn**" means "I'm planning" – that's enough in itself. What is important to us here though is that having broken "**dǎsuàn**" down into its component parts, we now have a new word to play with: "**suàn**", which means "count". Let's use it!

First though, what is "I'm planning"?

我打算
wǒ dǎsuàn
(wor dah-swann)

And what is "I hit"?

我打
wǒ dǎ
(wor dah)

And what is "count"?

算
suàn
(swann)

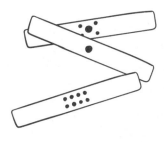

What is "not"?

不
bù
(boo)

So how would you say "not count"?

不算
bù suàn
(boo swann)

"That" in Chinese is:

那
nà
(nah)

So how would you say "That doesn't count" – literally "That not count"?

那不算。
Nà bù suàn.
(nah boo swann)

Now once again, what is "I hit"?

我打
wǒ dǎ
(wor dah)

And what is "I'm planning"?

我打算
wǒ dǎsuàn
(wor dah-swann)

And what is "count"?

算
suàn
(swann)

And what is "that"?

那
nà
(nah)

And so once more, how would you say "That doesn't count" / "That not count"?

那不算。
Nà bù suàn.
(nah boo swann)

"Erm" or "mmh" in Chinese is:

嗯
Ń
(ng[21])

---

[21]   This sounds very similar to the English "mmh" sound, except it's made with more of an "n" than an "m".

So how would you say "Erm, that doesn't count"?

嗯，那不算。
Ń, nà bù suàn.
(ng nah boo swann)

What is "I've been to China before"?

我去过中国。
Wǒ qù guò Zhōngguó.
(wor chü gwor ZHong-gwor)

And "You've been to China before"?

你去过中国。
Nǐ qù guò Zhōngguó.
(nee chü gwor ZHong-gwor)

And how about "Have you been to China before?"

你去过中国吗？
Nǐ qù guò Zhōngguó ma?
(nee chü gwor ZHong-gwor mah)

And what is "The Great Wall"?

长城
Chángchéng
(CHang-CHerng)

And what is "Chinatown"?

中国城
Zhōngguóchéng
(ZHong-gwor-cherng)

So how would you say "I've been to Chinatown before"?

我去过中国城。
Wǒ qù guò Zhōngguóchéng.
(wor chü gwor ZHong-gwor-cherng)

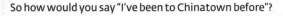

And again what is "erm" / "mmh"?

嗯
Ń
(ng)

So how would you say, "Erm, I've been to Chinatown before"?

嗯，我去过中国城。
Ń, wǒ qù guò Zhōngguóchéng.
(ng wor chü gwor ZHong-gwor-cherng)

What is "I'm planning"?

我打算
Wǒ dǎsuàn
(wor dah-swann)

And so how would you say "I'm planning to go to China"?

我打算去中国。
Wǒ dǎsuàn qù Zhōngguó.
(wor dah-swann chü ZHong-gwor)

And how about "I'm planning to go to China in May"?

我打算五月去中国。
Wǒ dǎsuàn wǔ yuè qù Zhōngguó.
(wor dah-swann woo yü-air chü ZHong-gwor)

What is "where"?

哪里
nǎlǐ
(nah-lee)

And so how would you say "Oh, whereabouts in China?"

喔，中国哪里？
Ō, Zhōngguó nǎlǐ?
(oh ZHong-gwor nah-lee)

What is "I don't know"?

我不知道。
Wǒ bù zhīdào.
(wor boo ZHi-dow)

And what is "yet"?

还
hái
(hy)

And so how would you say "I don't know yet"?

我还不知道。
Wǒ hái bù zhīdào.
(wor hy boo ZHi-dow)

What is "maybe"?

也许
yěxǔ
(ye-shü)

And what is "The Great Wall"?

长城
Chángchéng
(CHang-CHerng)

And so how would you say "I don't know yet. Maybe Shanghai, Beijing, The Great Wall"?

我还不知道，也许上海、北京、长城。
Wǒ hái bù zhīdào, yěxǔ Shànghǎi, Běijīng, Chángchéng.
(wor hy boo ZHi-dow ye-shü SHanghai bay-jing CHang-CHerng)

What is "I've been to China before"?

我去过中国。
Wǒ qù guò Zhōngguó.
(wor chü gwor ZHong-gwor)

How about "You've been to China before"?

你去过中国。
Nǐ qù guò Zhōngguó.
(nee chü gwor ZHong-gwor)

And "Have you been to China before?"

你去过中国吗？
Nǐ qù guò Zhōngguó ma?
(nee chü gwor ZHong-gwor mah)

Again, what is "Chinatown"?

中国城
Zhōngguóchéng
(ZHong-gwor-cherng)

And so how would you say "I've been to Chinatown before"?

我去过中国城。
Wǒ qù guò Zhōngguóchéng.
(wor chü gwor ZHong-gwor-cherng)

And how would you say "Erm, I've been to Chinatown before"?

嗯，我去过中国城。
Ń, wǒ qù guò Zhōngguóchéng.
(ng wor chü gwor ZHong-gwor-cherng)

What is "count"?

算
suàn
(swann)

And what is "that"?

那
nà
(nah)

And how would you say "That doesn't count"?

那不算！
Nà bù suàn!
(nah boo swann)

And how would you say "Mmh, that doesn't count"?

嗯，那不算！
Ń, nà bù suàn!
(ng nah boo swann)

Okay, you're now hopefully ready to make an attempt at doing the entire dialogue by yourself. Take each sentence slowly and, if you get it wrong, just take another stab at it. It isn't a race – instead just take your time to work it out.

Have a go now:

I'm planning to go to China in May.

我打算五月去中国。
Wǒ dǎsuàn wǔ yuè qù Zhōngguó.
(wor dah-swann woo yü-air chü ZHong-gwor)

Oh, whereabouts in China?

喔，中国哪里？
Ō, Zhōngguó nǎlǐ?
(oh ZHong-gwor nah-lee)

I don't know yet, maybe Shanghai, Beijing, The Great Wall.

我还不知道，也许上海、北京、长城。
Wǒ hái bù zhīdào, yěxǔ Shànghǎi, Běijīng, Chángchéng.
(wor hy boo ZHi-dow ye-shü SHanghai bay-jing CHang-CHerng)

Have you been before?

你去过吗？
Nǐ qù guò ma?
(*nee chü gwor mah*)

Erm, I've been to Chinatown.

嗯，我去过中国城。
Ń, wǒ qù guò Zhōngguóchéng.
(*ng wor chü gwor ZHong-gwor-cherng*)

Mmh, that doesn't count.

嗯，那不算！
Ń, nà bù suàn!
(*ng nah boo swann*)

Building Blocks 4

Okay. Building block time. Here they are:

As before, let's use the building blocks below to make as many sentences as we can. Make sure to use every word at least once and, preferably, several times!

173

well, off you go then!

你 **nǐ** (nee)	you
要 **yào** (yow)	want
你要 **Nǐ yào** (nee yow)	You want
炒 **chǎo** (CHow)	fried
面 **miàn** (mee-en)	noodles
炒面 **chǎo miàn** (CHow mee-en)	fried noodles / chow mein
你要炒面。 **Nǐ yào chǎo miàn.** (nee yow CHow mee-en)	You want fried noodles / chow mein.
豆腐 **dòufu** (doe-foo)	tofu
你要豆腐。 **Nǐ yào dòufu.** (nee yow doe-foo)	You want tofu.
吗？ **ma?** (mah)	spoken question mark

你要豆腐吗？ **Nǐ yào dòufu ma?** (nee yow doe-foo mah)	Do you want tofu?
和 **hé** (her)	and
你要炒面和豆腐吗？ **Nǐ yào chǎo miàn hé dòufu ma?** (nee yow CHow mee-en her doe-foo mah)	Do you want fried noodles and tofu?
饭 **fàn** (fan)	rice
炒饭 **chǎo fàn** (CHow fan)	fried rice
你要炒饭和豆腐吗？ **Nǐ yào chǎo fàn hé dòufu ma?** (nee yow CHow fan her doe-foo mah)	Do you want fried rice and tofu?
不 **bù** (boo)	not
你不要炒饭和豆腐吗？ **Nǐ bù yào chǎo fàn hé dòufu ma?** (nee boo yow CHow fan her doe-foo mah)	Don't you want fried rice and tofu?
我 **wǒ** (wor)	I
我要 **Wǒ yào** (wor yow)	I want
我要炒饭和豆腐。 **Wǒ yào chǎo fàn hé dòufu.** (wor yow CHow fan her doe-foo)	I want fried rice and tofu.
我不要 **Wǒ bù yào** (wor boo yow)	I don't want

我不要炒饭和豆腐。 **Wǒ bù yào chǎo fàn hé dòufu.** (wor boo yow CHow fan her doe-foo)	I don't want fried rice and tofu.
我知道。 **Wǒ zhīdào.** (wor ZHi-dow)	I know.
我知道你要炒面。 **Wǒ zhīdào nǐ yào chǎo miàn.** (wor ZHi-dow nee yow CHow mee-en)	I know you want fried noodles.
我不知道。 **Wǒ bù zhīdào.** (wor boo ZHi-dow)	I don't know.
也许 **yěxǔ** (ye-shü)	maybe
我不知道。也许。 **Wǒ bù zhīdào. Yěxǔ.** (wor boo ZHi-dow. ye-shü)	I don't know. Maybe.
一点 **yīdiǎn** (ee-dee-en)	a little / a bit of
咖啡 **kāfēi** (kah-fay)	coffee
她要 **Tā yào** (tah yow)	She wants
她要一点咖啡。 **Tā yào yīdiǎn kāfēi.** (tah yow ee-dee-en kah-fay)	She wants a little coffee.
她要一点咖啡吗？ **Tā yào yīdiǎn kāfēi ma?** (tah yow ee-dee-en kah-fay mah)	Does she want a little coffee?
他要 **Tā yào** (tah yow)	He wants

茶 **chá** (CHah)	tea
他要一点茶。 **Tā yào yīdiǎn chá.** (tah yow ee-dee-en CHah)	He wants a little tea.
他要一点茶吗？ **Tā yào yīdiǎn chá ma?** (tah yow ee-dee-en CHah mah)	Does he want a little tea?
他要一点炒饭吗？ **Tā yào yīdiǎn chǎo fàn ma?** (tah yow ee-dee-en CHow fan mah)	Does he want a bit of fried rice?
多一点 **duō yīdiǎn** (dwor ee-dee-en)	a bit more / a little more
他要多一点炒饭吗？ **Tā yào duō yīdiǎn chǎo fàn ma?** (tah yow dwor ee-dee-en CHow fan mah)	Does he want a bit more fried rice?
可乐 **kělè** (ker-ler)	cola / coke
他要多一点可乐吗？ **Tā yào duō yīdiǎn kělè ma?** (tah yow dwor ee-dee-en ker-ler mah)	Does he want a little more coke?
点心 **diǎnxīn** (dee-en-syin)	snack
她要点心。 **Tā yào diǎnxīn.** (tah yow dee-en-syin)	She wants a snack.
广式 **guǎng shì** (gwung SHi)	Cantonese-style
广式点心 **guǎng shì diǎnxīn** (gwung SHi dee-en-syin)	dim sum / Cantonese-style snack

她要广式点心。 **Tā yào guǎng shì diǎnxīn.** (tah yow gwung SHi dee-en-syin)	She wants dim sum.
点 **diǎn** (dee-en)	dot / point / order
我点 **Wǒ diǎn** (wor dee-en)	I order
我点了 **Wǒ diǎn le** (wor dee-en luh)	I ordered
我点了茶、咖啡和广式点心。 **Wǒ diǎn le chá, kāfēi hé guǎng shì diǎnxīn.** (wor dee-en luh CHah, kah-fay her gwung SHi dee-en-syin)	I ordered tea, coffee, and dim sum.
钱 **qián** (chee-en)	money
付钱 **fù qián** (foo chee-en)	pay (literally "pay money")
你付钱 **Nǐ fù qián** (nee foo chee-en)	You pay
你付了钱 **Nǐ fù le qián** (nee foo luh chee-en)	You paid
你付了钱吗？ **Nǐ fù le qián ma?** (nee foo luh chee-en mah)	Did you pay?
没 **méi** (may)	didn't

他没付钱 **Tā méi fù qián** (tah may foo chee-en)	He didn't pay
但是 **dànshì** (dan-SHi)	but
他点了茶、咖啡和广式点心，但是他没付钱！ **Tā diǎn le chá, kāfēi hé guǎng shì diǎnxīn, dànshì tā méi fù qián!** (tah dee-en luh CHah, kah-fay her gwung SHi dee-en-syin dan-SHi tah may foo chee-en)	He ordered tea, coffee, and dim sum but he didn't pay!
他们 **tāmen** (tah-men)	they
披萨 **pīsà** (pee-sa)	pizza
他们点了披萨，但是他们没付钱！ **Tāmen diǎn le pīsà, dànshì tāmen méi fù qián!** (tah-men dee-en luh pee-sa dan-SHi tah-men may foo chee-en)	They ordered pizza but they didn't pay!
吃 **chī** (CH)	eat
他们吃 **Tāmen chī** (tah-men CH)	They eat
他们吃了 **Tāmen chī le** (tah-men CH luh)	They ate
咕噜肉 **gūlū ròu** (goo-loo-roe)	sweet and sour pork

他们吃了咕噜肉。 **Tāmen chī le gūlū ròu.** (tah-men CH luh *goo-loo-roe*)	They ate sweet and sour pork.
我们 **wǒmen** (*wor-men*)	we
我们没吃咕噜肉。我们吃了披萨。 **Wǒmen méi chī gūlū ròu. Wǒmen chī le pīsà.** (*wor-men* may CH *goo-loo-roe. Wor-men* CH luh *pee-sa*)	We didn't eat sweet and sour pork. We ate pizza.
买 **mǎi** (*my*)	buy
我们买了咖啡。 **Wǒmen mǎi le kāfēi.** (*wor-men my* luh kah-fay)	We bought coffee.
我们买了咖啡。他们买了披萨。 **Wǒmen mǎi le kāfēi. Tāmen mǎi le pīsà.** (*wor-men my* luh kah-fay. Tah-men *my* luh *pee-sa*)	We bought coffee. They bought pizza.
去 **qù** (*chü*)	go / go to / to go to
我们去 **Wǒmen qù** (*wor-men chü*)	We go / We go to
我们去了 **Wǒmen qù le** (*wor-men chü* luh)	We went / We went to
上海 **Shànghǎi** (*SHanghai*)	Shanghai

北京 **Běijīng** (bay-jing)	Beijing
我们去了上海，但是他们 去了北京。 **Wǒmen qù le Shànghǎi, dànshì tāmen qù le Běijīng.** (wor-men chü luh SHanghai dan-SHi tah-men chü luh bay-jing)	We went to Shanghai but they went to Beijing.
打 **dǎ** (dah)	hit
麻将 **májiàng** (mah-jang)	mahjong
她打麻将。 **Tā dǎ májiàng.** (tah dah mah-jang)	She plays mahjong – literally "She hits mahjong".
她打了麻将。 **Tā dǎ le májiàng.** (tah dah luh mah-jang)	She played mahjong.
她打了麻将吗？ **Tā dǎ le májiàng ma?** (tah dah luh mah-jang mah)	Did she play mahjong?
我的 **wǒde** (wor-duh)	my
我的钱 **wǒde qián** (wor-duh chee-en)	my money
哪里？ **Nǎlǐ?** (nah-lee)	Where?
我的钱去了哪里？ **Wǒde qián qù le nǎlǐ?** (wor-duh chee-en chü luh nah-lee)	Where did my money go?

你的 **nǐde** (nee-duh)	your
你的钱去了哪里？ **Nǐde qián qù le nǎlǐ?** (nee-duh chee-en chü luh nah-lee)	Where did your money go?
我们去了上海，打了麻将。 **Wǒmen qù le Shànghǎi, dǎ le májiàng.** (wor-men chü luh SHanghai, dah luh mah-jang)	We went to Shanghai and played mahjong.
学了 **xué le** (shüwair luh)	learned / studied
功夫 **gōng fū** (gong foo)	kung fu
我们学了功夫。 **Wǒmen xué le gōng fū.** (wor-men shüwair luh gong foo)	We learned kung fu.
太极 **tàijí** (ty-jee)	tai chi
我们学了功夫，但是他们学了太极。 **Wǒmen xué le gōng fū, dànshì tāmen xué le tàijí.** (wor-men shüwair luh gong foo dan-SHi tah-men shüwair luh ty-jee)	We learned kung fu but they learned tai chi.
你们 **nǐmen** (nee-men)	you (MTOP)
你们学了太极吗？ **Nǐmen xué le tàijí ma?** (nee-men shüwair luh ty-jee mah)	Did you learn tai chi? (MTOP)

中文 **Zhōngwén** (ZHong-wen)	Chinese
你们学了中文吗? **Nǐmen xué le Zhōngwén ma?** (nee-men shüwair luh ZHong-wen mah)	Did you learn Chinese? (MTOP)
英文 **Yīngwén** (ying-wen)	English
你们学了英文吗? **Nǐmen xué le Yīngwén ma?** (nee-men shüwair luh ying-wen mah)	Did you learn English? (MTOP)
中 **zhōng** (ZHong)	Middle
国 **guó** (gwor)	Country / Kingdom
中国 **Zhōngguó** (ZHong-gwor)	China / Middle Country / Middle Kingdom
他们去了中国。 **Tāmen qù le Zhōngguó.** (tah-men chü luh ZHong-gwor)	They went to China.
他们去了中国吗? **Tāmen qù le Zhōngguó ma?** (tah-men chü luh ZHong-gwor mah)	Did they go to China?
我打算… **Wǒ dǎsuàn…** (wor dah-swann)	I'm planning to…
我打算去中国。 **Wǒ dǎsuàn qù Zhōngguó.** (wor dah-swann chü ZHong-gwor)	I'm planning to go to China.
五 **wǔ** (woo)	five

月 **yuè** (yü-air)	month
五月 **wǔ yuè** (woo yü-air)	May
我打算五月去中国。 **Wǒ dǎsuàn wǔ yuè qù Zhōngguó.** (wor dah-swann woo yü-air chü ZHong-gwor)	I'm planning to go to China in May.
喔 **Ō** (oh)	Oh!
喔，中国哪里？ **Ō, Zhōngguó nǎlǐ?** (oh ZHong-gwor nah-lee)	Oh, whereabouts in China?
还 **hái** (hy)	yet
我还不知道。 **Wǒ hái bù zhīdào.** (wor hy boo ZHi-dow)	I don't know yet.
长城 **Chángchéng** (CHang-CHerng)	The Great Wall
我还不知道，也许上海、 北京、长城。 **Wǒ hái bù zhīdào, yěxǔ Shànghǎi, Běijīng, Chángchéng.** (wor hy boo ZHi-dow ye-shü SHanghai bay-jing CHang-CHerng)	I don't know yet. Maybe Shanghai, Beijing, The Great Wall.
中国城 **Zhōngguóchéng** (ZHong-gwor-cherng)	Chinatown

去过 **qù guò** (chü gwor)	gone before / been before
你去过中国城吗? **Nǐ qù guò Zhōngguóchéng ma?** (nee chü gwor ZHong-gwor-cherng mah)	Have you been to Chinatown before?
吃过 **chī guò** (CH gwor)	eaten before
你吃过咕噜肉吗? **Nǐ chī guò gūlū ròu ma?** (nee CH gwor goo-loo-roe mah)	Have you eaten sweet and sour pork before?
一 **yī** (ee)	one
一月 **yī yuè** (ee yü-air)	January
新加坡 **Xīnjiāpō** (syin-jah-pwor)	Singapore
我打算一月去新加坡。 **Wǒ dǎsuàn yī yuè qù Xīnjiāpō.** (wor dah-swann ee yü-air chü syin-jah-pwor)	I'm planning to go to Singapore in January.
嗯 **Ń** (ng)	Erm
那 **nà** (nah)	that
算 **suàn** (swann)	count

嗯，那不算！ **Ń, nà bù suàn!** (ng nah boo swann)	Erm, that doesn't count.
需要 **xūyào** (shü-yow)	need
明天 **míngtiān** (ming-tee-en)	tomorrow
早上 **zǎoshang** (zow-SHang)	morning
台湾 **Táiwān** (taiwan)	Taiwan
他们需要明天早上去台湾。 **Tāmen xūyào míngtiān zǎoshang qù Táiwān.** (tah-men shü-yow ming-tee-en zow-SHang chü taiwan)	They need to go to Taiwan tomorrow morning.
今天 **jīntiān** (jin-tee-en)	today
晚上 **wǎnshang** (wun-SHang)	evening
今天晚上 **jīntiān wǎnshang** (jin-tee-en wun-SHang)	this evening
我们需要今天晚上去中国城。 **Wǒmen xūyào jīntiān wǎnshang qù Zhōngguóchéng.** (wor-men shü-yow jin-tee-en wun-SHang chü ZHong-gwor-cherng)	We need to go to Chinatown this evening.

Now, time to do it the other way around!

you	你 **nǐ** (nee)
want	要 **yào** (yow)
You want	你要 **Nǐ yào** (nee yow)
fried	炒 **chǎo** (CHow)
noodles	面 **miàn** (mee-en)
fried noodles / chow mein	炒面 **chǎo miàn** (CHow mee-en)
You want fried noodles / chow mein.	你要炒面。 **Nǐ yào chǎo miàn.** (nee yow CHow mee-en)
tofu	豆腐 **dòufu** (doe-foo)
You want tofu.	你要豆腐。 **Nǐ yào dòufu.** (nee yow doe-foo)
spoken question mark	吗？ **ma?** (mah)
Do you want tofu?	你要豆腐吗？ **Nǐ yào dòufu ma?** (nee yow doe-foo mah)

and	和 **hé** (her)
Do you want fried noodles and tofu?	你要炒面和豆腐吗？ **Nǐ yào chǎo miàn hé dòufu ma?** (nee yow CHow mee-en her doe-foo mah)
rice	饭 **fàn** (fan)
fried rice	炒饭 **chǎo fàn** (CHow fan)
Do you want fried rice and tofu?	你要炒饭和豆腐吗？ **Nǐ yào chǎo fàn hé dòufu ma?** (nee yow CHow fan her doe-foo mah)
not	不 **bù** (boo)
Don't you want fried rice and tofu?	你不要炒饭和豆腐吗？ **Nǐ bù yào chǎo fàn hé dòufu ma?** (nee boo yow CHow fan her doe-foo mah)
I	我 **wǒ** (wor)
I want	我要 **Wǒ yào** (wor yow)
I want fried rice and tofu.	我要炒饭和豆腐。 **Wǒ yào chǎo fàn hé dòufu.** (wor yow CHow fan her doe-foo)
I don't want	我不要 **Wǒ bù yào** (wor boo yow)
I don't want fried rice and tofu.	我不要炒饭和豆腐。 **Wǒ bù yào chǎo fàn hé dòufu.** (wor boo yow CHow fan her doe-foo)

I know.	我知道。 **Wǒ zhīdào.** (wor ZHi-dow)
I know you want fried noodles.	我知道你要炒面。 **Wǒ zhīdào nǐ yào chǎo miàn.** (wor ZHi-dow nee yow CHow mee-en)
I don't know.	我不知道。 **Wǒ bù zhīdào.** (wor boo ZHi-dow)
maybe	也许 **yěxǔ** (ye-shü)
I don't know. Maybe.	我不知道。也许。 **Wǒ bù zhīdào. Yěxǔ.** (wor boo ZHi-dow. ye-shü)
a little / a bit of	一点 **yīdiǎn** (ee-dee-en)
coffee	咖啡 **kāfēi** (kah-fay)
She wants	她要 **Tā yào** (tah yow)
She wants a little coffee.	她要一点咖啡。 **Tā yào yīdiǎn kāfēi.** (tah yow ee-dee-en kah-fay)
Does she want a little coffee?	她要一点咖啡吗？ **Tā yào yīdiǎn kāfēi ma?** (tah yow ee-dee-en kah-fay mah)
He wants	他要 **Tā yào** (tah yow)
tea	茶 **chá** (CHah)

He wants a little tea.	他要一点茶。 **Tā yào yīdiǎn chá.** (tah yow ee-dee-en CHah)
Does he want a little tea?	他要一点茶吗？ **Tā yào yīdiǎn chá ma?** (tah yow ee-dee-en CHah mah)
Does he want a bit of fried rice?	他要一点炒饭吗？ **Tā yào yīdiǎn chǎo fàn ma?** (tah yow ee-dee-en CHow fan mah)
a bit more / a little more	多一点 **duō yīdiǎn** (dwor ee-dee-en)
Does he want a bit more fried rice?	他要多一点炒饭吗？ **Tā yào duō yīdiǎn chǎo fàn ma?** (tah yow dwor ee-dee-en CHow fan mah)
cola / coke	可乐 **kělè** (ker-ler)
Does he want a little more coke?	他要多一点可乐吗？ **Tā yào duō yīdiǎn kělè ma?** (tah yow dwor ee-dee-en ker-ler mah)
snack	点心 **diǎnxīn** (dee-en-syin)
She wants a snack.	她要点心。 **Tā yào diǎnxīn.** (tah yow dee-en-syin)
Cantonese-style	广式 **guǎng shì** (gwung SHi)
dim sum / Cantonese-style snack	广式点心 **guǎng shì diǎnxīn** (gwung SHi dee-en-syin)
She wants dim sum.	她要广式点心。 **Tā yào guǎng shì diǎnxīn.** (tah yow gwung SHi dee-en-syin)

dot / point / order	点 **diǎn** (dee-en)
I order	我点 **Wǒ diǎn** (wor dee-en)
I ordered	我点了 **Wǒ diǎn le** (wor dee-en luh)
I ordered tea, coffee, and dim sum.	我点了茶、咖啡和广式点心。 **Wǒ diǎn le chá, kāfēi hé guǎng shì diǎnxīn.** (wor dee-en luh CHah, kah-fay her gwung SHi dee-en-syin)
money	钱 **qián** (chee-en)
pay (literally "pay money")	付钱 **fù qián** (foo chee-en)
You pay	你付钱 **Nǐ fù qián** (nee foo chee-en)
You paid	你付了钱 **Nǐ fù le qián** (nee foo luh chee-en)
Did you pay?	你付了钱吗? **Nǐ fù le qián ma?** (nee foo luh chee-en mah)
didn't	没 **méi** (may)
He didn't pay	他没付钱 **Tā méi fù qián** (tah may foo chee-en)

but	但是
	dànshì
	(dan-SHi)

He ordered tea, coffee, and dim sum but he didn't pay!	他点了茶、咖啡和广式点心，但是他没付钱！
	Tā diǎn le chá, kāfēi hé guǎng shì diǎnxīn, dànshì tā méi fù qián!
	(tah dee-en luh CHah, kah-fay her gwung SHi dee-en-syin dan-SHi tah may foo chee-en)

they	他们
	tāmen
	(tah-men)

pizza	披萨
	pīsà
	(pee-sa)

They ordered pizza but they didn't pay!	他们点了披萨，但是他们没付钱！
	Tāmen diǎn le pīsà, dànshì tāmen méi fù qián!
	(tah-men dee-en luh pee-sa dan-SHi tah-men may foo chee-en)

eat	吃
	chī
	(CH)

They eat	他们吃
	Tāmen chī
	(tah-men CH)

They ate	他们吃了
	Tāmen chī le
	(tah-men CH luh)

Sweet and sour pork	咕噜肉
	gūlū ròu
	(goo-loo-roe)

They ate sweet and sour pork.	他们吃了咕噜肉。
	Tāmen chī le gūlū ròu.
	(tah-men CH luh goo-loo-roe)

we	我们 **wǒmen** (wor-men)
We didn't eat sweet and sour pork. We ate pizza.	我们没吃咕噜肉。我们吃了 披萨。 **Wǒmen méi chī gūlū ròu.** **Wǒmen chī le pīsà.** (wor-men may CH goo-loo-roe. Wor-men CH luh pee-sa)
buy	买 **mǎi** (my)
We bought coffee.	我们买了咖啡。 **Wǒmen mǎi le kāfēi.** (wor-men my luh kah-fay)
We bought coffee. They bought pizza.	我们买了咖啡。他们买了 披萨。 **Wǒmen mǎi le kāfēi. Tāmen mǎi** **le pīsà.** (wor-men my luh kah-fay. Tah-men my luh pee-sa)
go / go to / to go to	去 **qù** (chü)
We go / We go to	我们去 **Wǒmen qù** (wor-men chü)
We went / We went to	我们去了 **Wǒmen qù le** (wor-men chü luh)
Shanghai	上海 **Shànghǎi** (SHanghai)
Beijing	北京 **Běijīng** (bay-jing)

We went to Shanghai but they went to Beijing.	我们去了上海，但是他们去了北京。 **Wǒmen qù le Shànghǎi, dànshì tāmen qù le Běijīng.** (wor-men chü luh SHanghai dan-SHi tah-men chü luh bay-jing)
hit	打 **dǎ** (dah)
mahjong	麻将 **májiàng** (mah-jang)
She plays mahjong – literally "She hits mahjong".	她打麻将。 **Tā dǎ májiàng.** (tah dah mah-jang)
She played mahjong.	她打了麻将。 **Tā dǎ le májiàng.** (tah dah luh mah-jang)
Did she play mahjong?	她打了麻将吗？ **Tā dǎ le májiàng ma?** (tah dah luh mah-jang mah)
my	我的 **wǒde** (wor-duh)
my money	我的钱 **wǒde qián** (wor-duh chee-en)
Where?	哪里？ **Nǎlǐ?** (nah-lee)
Where did my money go?	我的钱去了哪里？ **Wǒde qián qù le nǎlǐ?** (wor-duh chee-en chü luh nah-lee)
your	你的 **nǐde** (nee-duh)

Where did your money go?	你的钱去了哪里？ **Nǐde qián qù le nǎlǐ?** (nee-duh chee-en chü luh nah-lee)
We went to Shanghai and played mahjong.	我们去了上海，打了麻将。 **Wǒmen qù le Shànghǎi, dǎ le mǎjiàng.** (wor-men chü luh SHanghai, dah luh mah-jang)
learned / studied	学了 **xué le** (shüwair luh)
kung fu	功夫 **gōng fū** (gong foo)
We learned kung fu.	我们学了功夫。 **Wǒmen xué le gōng fū.** (wor-men shüwair luh gong foo)
tai chi	太极 **tàijí** (ty-jee)
We learned kung fu but they learned tai chi.	我们学了功夫，但是他们学了太极。 **Wǒmen xué le gōng fū, dànshì tāmen xué le tàijí.** (wor-men shüwair luh gong foo dan-SHi tah-men shüwair luh ty-jee)
you (MTOP)	你们 **nǐmen** (nee-men)
Did you learn tai chi? (MTOP)	你们学了太极吗？ **Nǐmen xué le tàijí ma?** (nee-men shüwair luh ty-jee mah)
Chinese	中文 **Zhōngwén** (ZHong-wen)

Did you learn Chinese? (MTOP)	你们学了中文吗？ **Nǐmen xué le Zhōngwén ma?** *(nee-men shüwair luh ZHong-wen mah)*
English	英文 **Yīngwén** *(ying-wen)*
Did you learn English? (MTOP)	你们学了英文吗？ **Nǐmen xué le Yīngwén ma?** *(nee-men shüwair luh ying-wen mah)*
Middle	中 **zhōng** *(ZHong)*
Country / Kingdom	国 **guó** *(gwor)*
China / Middle Country / Middle Kingdom	中国 **Zhōngguó** *(ZHong-gwor)*
They went to China.	他们去了中国。 **Tāmen qù le Zhōngguó.** *(tah-men chü luh ZHong-gwor)*
Did they go to China?	他们去了中国吗？ **Tāmen qù le Zhōngguó ma?** *(tah-men chü luh ZHong-gwor mah)*
I'm planning to…	我打算… **Wǒ dǎsuàn…** *(wor dah-swann)*
I'm planning to go to China.	我打算去中国。 **Wǒ dǎsuàn qù Zhōngguó.** *(wor dah-swann chü ZHong-gwor)*
five	五 **wǔ** *(woo)*
month	月 **yuè** *(yü-air)*

May	五月 **wǔ yuè** (woo yü-air)
I'm planning to go to China in May.	我打算五月去中国。 **Wǒ dǎsuàn wǔ yuè qù Zhōngguó.** (wor dah-swann woo yü-air chü ZHong-gwor)
Oh!	喔 **Ō** (oh)
Oh, whereabouts in China?	喔，中国哪里？ **Ō, Zhōngguó nǎlǐ?** (oh ZHong-gwor nah-lee)
yet	还 **hái** (hy)
I don't know yet.	我还不知道。 **Wǒ hái bù zhīdào.** (wor hy boo ZHi-dow)
The Great Wall	长城 **Chángchéng** (CHang-CHerng)
I don't know yet. Maybe Shanghai, Beijing, The Great Wall.	我还不知道，也许上海、北京、长城。 **Wǒ hái bù zhīdào, yěxǔ Shànghǎi, Běijīng, Chángchéng.** (wor hy boo ZHi-dow ye-shü SHanghai bay-jing CHang-CHerng)
Chinatown	中国城 **Zhōngguóchéng** (ZHong-gwor-cherng)
gone before / been before	去过 **qù guò** (chü gwor)

Have you been to Chinatown before?	你去过中国城吗？ **Nǐ qù guò Zhōngguóchéng ma?** (nee chü gwor ZHong-gwor-cherng mah)
eaten before	吃过 **chī guò** (CH gwor)
Have you eaten sweet and sour pork before?	你吃过咕噜肉吗？ **Nǐ chī guò gūlū ròu ma?** (nee CH gwor goo-loo-roe mah?)
one	一 **yī** (ee)
January	一月 **yī yuè** (ee yü-air)
Singapore	新加坡 **Xīnjiāpō** (syin-jah-pwor)
I'm planning to go to Singapore in January.	我打算一月去新加坡。 **Wǒ dǎsuàn yī yuè qù Xīnjiāpō.** (wor dah-swann ee yü-air chü syin-jah-pwor)
Erm	嗯 **Ń** (ng)
that	那 **nà** (nah)
count	算 **suàn** (swann)
Erm, that doesn't count.	嗯，那不算！ **Ń, nà bù suàn!** (ng nah boo swann)
need	需要 **xūyào** (shü-yow)

tomorrow	明天 **míngtiān** (ming-tee-en)
morning	早上 **zǎoshang** (zow-SHang)
Taiwan	台湾 **Táiwān** (taiwan)
They need to go to Taiwan tomorrow morning.	他们需要明天早上去台湾。 **Tāmen xūyào míngtiān zǎoshang qù Táiwān.** (tah-men shü-yow ming-tee-en zow-SHang chü taiwan)
today	今天 **jīntiān** (jin-tee-en)
evening	晚上 **wǎnshang** (wun-SHang)
this evening	今天晚上 **jīntiān wǎnshang** (jin-tee-en wun-SHang)
We need to go to Chinatown this evening.	我们需要今天晚上去中国城。 **Wǒmen xūyào jīntiān wǎnshang qù Zhōngguóchéng.** (wor-men shü-yow jin-tee-en wun-SHang chü ZHong-gwor-cherng)

Well, that's it, you're done with Chapter 4! Remember, don't try to hold onto or remember anything you've learned here. Everything you learned in earlier chapters will be brought back up and reinforced later on. You don't need to do anything or make any effort to memorise anything.

Forget what you were taught at school!

Many of us were told at school that we did not have an aptitude for languages, that we didn't have a "knack" or a "gift" for them.

Well, if this applies to you, then please let me assure you that this is all absolute nonsense! If you are able to read these words in front of you then this demonstrates that you've been able to learn English and, if you can learn one language, then your brain is just as capable of learning another – it simply needs to be approached in the right way!

In fact, since you've got as far as the end of Chapter 4, it should already be obvious to you that you are quite capable of learning a foreign language when it's taught in the right way. The secret to success for you will be choosing the right materials once you're finished with this book (more on that later).

CHAPTER 5

You know what?
She won all my
money!

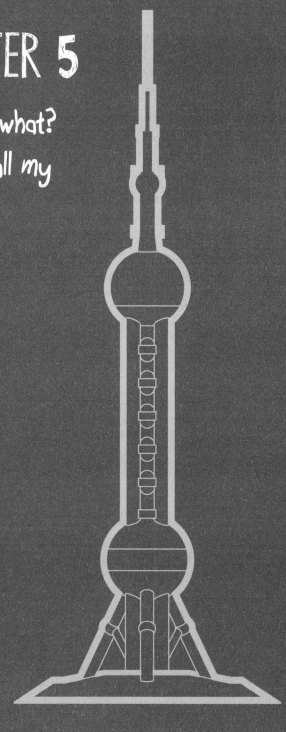

I need a little more time.
Why?
Because I didn't eat dinner yet.
Oh, why not?
Because my mum came over and we played mahjong.
You know what? She won all my money!

Mums! What are they like, eh?! Either they're ringing you up complaining you never visit them or they're popping over and cleaning you out financially.

Well, the sentences above will not only allow you to report such behaviour but they're also going to introduce some crucial Chinese vocabulary. Let's get building them!

What is "I want"?

我要
wǒ yào
(wor yow)

And how would you say "I want fried rice"?

我要炒饭。
Wǒ yào chǎo fàn.
(wor yow CHow fan)

What is "sweet and sour pork"?

咕噜肉
gūlū ròu
(goo-loo-roe)

And what is "and"?

和
hé
(her)

So how would you say "I want sweet and sour pork and fried rice"?

我要咕噜肉和炒饭。
Wǒ yào gūlū ròu hé chǎo fàn.
(wor yow goo-loo roe her CHow fan)

What is "a bit of" / "a little"?

一点
yīdiǎn
(ee-dee-en)

And do you remember how to say "a little more"?

多一点
duō yīdiǎn
(dwor ee-dee-en)

How about "a little more fried rice"?

多一点炒饭
duō yīdiǎn chǎo fàn
(dwor ee-dee-en CHow fan)

And so how would you say "I want a little more fried rice"?

我要多一点炒饭。
Wǒ yào duō yīdiǎn chǎo fàn.
(wor yow dwor ee-dee-en CHow fan)

Again, what is "I need"?

我需要
wǒ xūyào
(wor shü-yow)

So how would you say "I need a little more fried rice"?

我需要多一点炒饭。
Wǒ xūyào duō yīdiǎn chǎo fàn.
(wor shü-yow dwor ee-dee-en CHow fan)

How about "I need a little more tea"?

我需要多一点茶。
Wǒ xūyào duō yīdiǎn chá.
(wor shü-yow dwor ee-dee-en CHah)

"Time" in Chinese is:

时间
shíjiān
(SHi-jee-en)

So how would you say "I need a little more time"?

我需要多一点时间。
Wǒ xūyào duō yīdiǎn shíjiān.
(wor shü-yow dwor ee-dee-en SHi-jee-en)

How about "You need a little more time"?

你需要多一点时间。
Nǐ xūyào duō yīdiǎn shíjiān.
(nee shü-yow dwor ee-dee-en SHi-jee-en)

And "Do you need a little more time?"

你需要多一点时间吗？
Nǐ xūyào duō yīdiǎn shíjiān ma?
(nee shü-yow dwor ee-dee-en SHi-jee-en mah)

What is "I go"?

我去
wǒ qù
(wor chü)

And what is "didn't"?

没
méi
(may)

So how would you say "I didn't go"?

我没去。
Wǒ méi qù.
(wor may chü)

What is "I eat"?

我吃
wǒ chī
(wor CH)

And so how would you say "I didn't eat"?

我没吃。
Wǒ méi chī.
(wor may CH)

What is "yet"?

还
hái
(hy)

To say "I didn't eat yet" – you'll literally say "I yet didn't eat." How would you say that?

我还没吃。
Wǒ hái méi chī.
(wor hy may CH)

Do you remember how to say "evening"?

晚上
wǎnshang
(wun-SHang)

And literally that means "late on". As that's the case, what is "on" in Chinese?

上
shàng
(shang)

And what is "late"?

晚
wǎn
(wun)

What is "rice"?

饭
fàn
(fan)

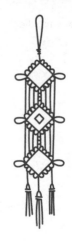

And so how would you say "late rice"?

晚饭
wǎnfàn
(wun fan)

And that's one way to say "dinner" in Chinese.

Now again, what was "I didn't eat"?

我没吃。
Wǒ méi chī.
(wor may CH)

And what was "dinner" – literally "late rice"?

晚饭
wǎnfàn
(wun fan)

And so how would you say "I didn't eat dinner"?

我没吃晚饭。
Wǒ méi chī wǎnfàn.
(wor may CH wun-fan)

How about "I didn't eat dinner yet" – literally "I yet didn't eat dinner"?

我还没吃晚饭。
Wǒ hái méi chī wǎnfàn.
(wor hy may CH wun-fan)

And how would you say "You didn't eat dinner yet"?

你还没吃晚饭。
Nǐ hái méi chī wǎnfàn.
(nee hy may CH wun-fan)

And what about "Didn't you eat dinner yet?" – literally "You yet didn't eat dinner ma?"

你还没吃晚饭吗？
Nǐ hái méi chī wǎnfàn ma?
(nee hy may CH wun-fan mah)

Again, what was "I need"?

我需要
wǒ xūyào
(wor shü-yow)

And as you may remember, "time" in Chinese is:

时间
shíjiān
(SHi-jee-en)

So how would you say "I need time"?

我需要时间。
Wǒ xūyào shíjiān.
(wor shü-yow SHi-jee-en)

And how would you say "I need a little more time"?

我需要多一点时间。
Wǒ xūyào duō yīdiǎn shíjiān.
(wor shü-yow dwor ee-dee-en SHi-jee-en)

What is "evening" – literally "late on"?

晚上
wǎnshang
(wun-SHang)

And what is "dinner"?

晚饭
wǎnfàn
(wun-fan)

And again, how would you say "I didn't eat dinner yet"?

我还没吃晚饭。
Wǒ hái méi chī wǎnfàn.
(wor hy may CH wun-fan)

What is "my"?

我的
wǒde
(wor-duh)

And so how would you say "my money"?

我的钱
wǒde qián
(wor-duh chee-en)

"Mum/ Mom[22]" in Chinese is:

妈妈
māma
(mah-mah)

So how would you say "my mum"?

我的妈妈
wǒde māma
(wor-duh mah-mah)

And how would you say "my mum goes"?

我的妈妈去
wǒde māma qù
(wor-duh mah-mah chü)

---

22 A fun British / American language difference here. If you're American and reading this book, please be aware that British people spell "mom" as "mum" and this is what I do throughout the book. So, if you're from the U.S. please just read all instances of "mum" you find here as "mom"!

And "my mum went"?

我的妈妈去了
wǒde māma qù le
(wor-duh mah-mah chü luh)

How about "My mum went to The Great Wall"?

我的妈妈去了长城。
Wǒde māma qù le Chángchéng.
(wor-duh mah-mah chü luh CHang-CHerng)

"Come" or "come over" in Chinese is:

来
lái
(ly[23])

So how would you say "I come" / "I come over"?

我来
wǒ lái
(wor ly)

And how would you say "my mum comes" / "my mum comes over"?

我的妈妈来
wǒde māma lái
(wor-duh mah-mah ly)

And how do you think you'd say "my mum came" / "my mum came over"?

我的妈妈来了
wǒde māma lái le
(wor-duh mah-mah ly luh)

And how about "Did my mum come?" / "Did my mum come over?"

我的妈妈来了吗？
Wǒde māma lái le ma?
(wor-duh mah-mah ly luh mah)

---

23 Pronounced like the "ly" in the English words "lycra" and "lychee".

What about "Did they come?" / "Did they come over?"

他们来了吗？
Tāmen lái le ma?
(tah-men ly luh mah)

What is "I need"?

我需要
wǒ xūyào
(wor shü-yow)

And so how would you say "I need to come"?

我需要来。
Wǒ xūyào lái.
(wor shü-yow ly)

What is "time"?

时间
shíjiān
(SHi-jee-en)

So how would you say "I need to come but I need time"?

我需要来，但是我需要时间。
Wǒ xūyào lái, dànshì wǒ xūyào shíjiān.
(wor shü-yow ly dan-SHi wor shü-yow SHi-jee-en)

"Win" in Chinese is:

赢
yíng
(ing)

So how would you say "I win"?

我赢
wǒ yíng
(wor ing)

How about "she wins"?

她赢
tā yíng
(tah ing)

And how do you think you'd say "she won"?

她赢了
tā yíng le
(tah ing luh)

And so how would you say "She won my money"?

她赢了我的钱。
Tā yíng le wǒde qián.
(tah ing luh wor-duh chee-en)

How about "They won my money"?

他们赢了我的钱。
Tāmen yíng le wǒde qián.
(tah-men ing luh wor-duh chee-en)

"All my money" in Chinese would be:

我所有的钱
wǒ suǒyǒu de qián
(wor swore-yoe duh chee-en)

Notice how the "all" is put in the middle of the word meaning "my".

So how would you say, "They won all my money"?

他们赢了我所有的钱。
Tāmen yíng le wǒ suǒyǒu de qián.
(tah-men ing luh wor swore-yoe duh chee-en)

And how about "She won all my money"?

她赢了我所有的钱。
Tā yíng le wǒ suǒyǒu de qián.
(tah ing luh wor swore-yoe duh chee-en)

And how would you say "My mum came over. She won all of my money!"

我的妈妈来了。她赢了我所有的钱。
Wǒde māma lái le. Tā yíng le wǒ suǒyǒu de qián.
(wor-duh mah-mah ly luh. tah ing luh wor swore-yoe duh chee-en)

What is "hit"?

打
dǎ
(dah)

And so how would you say "We played mahjong"?

我们打了麻将。
Wǒmen dǎ le májiàng.
(wor-men dah luh mah-jang)

And how would you say "My mum came over and we played mahjong"?

我的妈妈来了。我们打了麻将。
Wǒde māma lái le. Wǒmen dǎ le májiàng.
(wor-duh mah-mah ly luh. wor-men dah luh mah-jang)

Did you remember that we leave out the "and" when we're using it to join two halves of a sentence together?

How about "My mum came over and we played mahjong. She won all my money!"?

我的妈妈来了。我们打了麻将。她赢了我所有的钱。
Wǒde māma lái le. Wǒmen dǎ le májiàng. Tā yíng le wǒ suǒyǒu de qián.
(wor-duh mah-mah ly luh. wor-men dah luh mah-jang. Tah ing luh wor swore-yoe duh chee-en)

"Why?" in Chinese is:

为什么？
Wèishénme?
(way-SHen-muh)

It literally means "for what?"

So how would you say, "Oh, why?"

喔，为什么？
Ō, wèishénme?
(oh way-SHen-muh)

Now again, how would someone say "I need a little more time"?

我需要多一点时间。
Wǒ xūyào duō yīdiǎn shíjiān.
(wor shü-yow dwor ee-dee-en SHi-jee-en)

And how would you respond to this, saying "Oh, why?"

喔，为什么？
Ō, wèishénme?
(oh way-SHen-muh)

What is "money"?

钱
qián
(chee-en)

So how would someone say "I need a little more money"?

我需要多一点钱。
Wǒ xūyào duō yīdiǎn qián.
(wor shü-yow dwor ee-dee-en chee-en)

And again how would you respond to this, saying "Oh, why?"

喔，为什么？
Ō, wèishénme?
(oh way-SHen-muh)

How would someone say "I didn't eat dinner yet"?

我还没吃晚饭。
Wǒ hái méi chī wǎnfàn.
(wor hy may CH wun-fan)

If you wanted to ask that person "Oh, why not?" you'd say "Oh, why yet didn't?" How would you say that?

喔，为什么还没？
Ō, wèishénme hái méi?
(oh way-SHen-muh hy may)

What is "order"?

点
diǎn
(dee-en)

So how would someone say "I didn't order dinner yet"?

我还没点晚饭。
Wǒ hái méi diǎn wǎnfàn.
(wor hy may dee-en wun-fan)

And again, how would you reply to that, asking "Oh, why not?"

喔，为什么还没？
Ō, wèishénme hái méi?
(oh way-SHen-muh hy may)

As I've mentioned before, "win" in Chinese is:

赢
yíng
(ing)

So again, how would you say "she won"?

她赢了
tā yíng le
(tah ing luh)

And "She won my money"?

她赢了我的钱。
Tā yíng le wǒde qián.
(tah ing luh wor-duh chee-en)

And as I've also mentioned, "all my money" in Chinese is:

我所有的钱
wǒ suǒyǒu de qián
(wor swore-yoe duh chee-en)

So how would you say "She won all my money?"

她赢了我所有的钱。
Tā yíng le wǒ suǒyǒu de qián.
(tah ing luh wor swore-yoe duh chee-en)

What is "Why?"

为什么
Wèishénme?
(way-SHen-muh)

And how would you say "Oh, why?"

喔，为什么？
Ō, wèishénme?
(oh way-SHen-muh)

And once again, how would someone say "I didn't eat dinner yet"?

我还没吃晚饭。
Wǒ hái méi chī wǎnfàn.
(wor hy may CH wun-fan)

And how would you reply to this saying "Oh, why not?" – literally
"Oh, why yet didn't?"

喔，为什么还没？
Ō, wèishénme hái méi?
(oh way-SHen-muh hy may)

Now, as I mentioned briefly earlier, why (wèishénme) literally means "for what?"
So which part means of that do you think means "for"?

为
wèi
(way)

"Because" in Chinese is:

因为
yīnwèi
(yin-way)

And literally this means "reason for" which kind of makes sense as "because" is used to give the "reason for" something.

So how would you say "because I didn't eat dinner yet"?

因为我还没吃晚饭。
Yīnwèi wǒ hái méi chī wǎnfàn.
(yin-way wor hy may CH wun-fan)

And how would you say "because I need a little more time"?

因为我需要多一点时间。
Yīnwèi wǒ xūyào duō yīdiǎn shíjiān.
(yin-way wor shü-yow dwor ee-dee-en SHi-jee-en)

And how would you say "because my mum came over and we played mahjong"?

因为我的妈妈来了。我们打了麻将。
Yīnwèi wǒde māma lái le. Wǒmen dǎ le májiàng.
(yin-way wor-duh mah-mah ly luh. wor-men dah luh mah-jang)

What is "you know"?

你知道
nǐ zhīdào
(nee ZHi-dow)

If you want to say to someone in Chinese "you know what?" you'll literally simply say "you know ma?" So, you just add the spoken question mark onto the end of "you know". Do that now. Say "you know what?"

你知道吗？
Nǐ zhīdào ma?
(nee ZHi-dow mah)

Now again, what was "She won all my money"?

她赢了我所有的钱。
Tā yíng le wǒ suǒyǒu de qián.
(tah ing luh wor swore-yoe duh chee-en)

And so now say "You know what? She won all my money!"

你知道吗？她赢了我所有的钱。
Nǐ zhīdào ma? Tā yíng le wǒ suǒyǒu de qián.
(nee ZHi-dow mah tah ing luh wor swore-yoe duh chee-en)

Okay, let's try to put all this together now and return to what was said at the beginning of the chapter. There was a lot covered here, so don't even begin to expect to get it all right the first time through. Instead, think of each attempt as a dress rehearsal, leading up to the perfect read-through on something like the eighth attempt.

Okay, ready? Let's do it!

I need a little more time.

我需要多一点时间。
Wǒ xūyào duō yīdiǎn shíjiān.
(wor shü-yow dwor ee-dee-en SHi-jee-en)

Why?

为什么？
Wèishénme?
(way-SHen-muh)

Because I didn't eat dinner yet.

因为我还没吃晚饭。
Yīnwèi wǒ hái méi chī wǎnfàn.
(yin-way wor hy may CH wun-fan)

Oh, why not?

喔，为什么还没？
Ō, wèishénme hái méi?
(oh way-SHen-muh hy may)

Because my mum / mom came over and we played mahjong. You know what? She won all my money!

因为我的妈妈来了。我们打了麻将。你知道吗？她赢了我所有的钱。

Yīnwèi wǒde māma lái le. Wǒmen dǎ le májiàng. Nǐ zhīdào ma? Tā yíng le wǒ suǒyǒu de qián.

(yin-way wor-duh mah-mah ly luh. wor-men dah luh mah-jang. Ni ZHi-dow mah. Tah ing luh wor swore-yoe duh chee-en)

How did that go? There's some fairly complex aspects of Chinese dealt with in there but as you're probably beginning to notice it is also just a matter of patterns. Learn the patterns and you'll find that you can very quickly begin to communicate in the language – and with a minimum of effort!

Final Checklist

Well, that's it! You've just finished your final chapter, which makes this your final checklist. Unlike the ones that came before it, however, you are not finished with this checklist until you can go the whole way through it without making a single mistake.

This doesn't mean that making mistakes when you go through it is a bad thing. It's just that I want you to return to it multiple times until going through the list becomes so easy that you can do so without making a single error.

When you can, it means you have really learned what I wanted to teach you in these pages.

Now, get to it!

你 **nǐ** (nee)	you
要 **yào** (yow)	want
你要 **Nǐ yào** (nee yow)	You want
炒 **chǎo** (CHow)	fried
面 **miàn** (mee-en)	noodles
炒面 **chǎo miàn** (CHow mee-en)	fried noodles / chow mein

你要炒面。 **Nǐ yào chǎo miàn.** (nee yow CHow mee-en)	You want fried noodles / chow mein.
豆腐 **dòufu** (doe-foo)	tofu
你要豆腐。 **Nǐ yào dòufu.** (nee yow doe-foo)	You want tofu.
吗? **ma?** (mah)	spoken question mark
你要豆腐吗? **Nǐ yào dòufu ma?** (nee yow doe-foo mah)	Do you want tofu?
和 **hé** (her)	and
你要炒面和豆腐吗? **Nǐ yào chǎo miàn hé dòufu ma?** (nee yow CHow mee-en her doe-foo mah)	Do you want fried noodles and tofu?
饭 **fàn** (fan)	rice
炒饭 **chǎo fàn** (CHow fan)	fried rice
你要炒饭和豆腐吗? **Nǐ yào chǎo fàn hé dòufu ma?** (nee yow CHow fan her doe-foo mah)	Do you want fried rice and tofu?
不 **bù** (boo)	not

你不要炒饭和豆腐吗？ **Nǐ bù yào chǎo fàn hé dòufu ma?** (nee *boo* yow CHow fan her *doe-foo* mah)	Don't you want fried rice and tofu?
我 **wǒ** (wor)	I
我要 **Wǒ yào** (wor yow)	I want
我要炒饭和豆腐。 **Wǒ yào chǎo fàn hé dòufu.** (wor yow CHow fan her *doe-foo*)	I want fried rice and tofu.
我不要 **Wǒ bù yào** (wor *boo* yow)	I don't want
我不要炒饭和豆腐。 **Wǒ bù yào chǎo fàn hé dòufu.** (wor *boo* yow CHow fan her *doe-foo*)	I don't want fried rice and tofu.
我知道。 **Wǒ zhīdào.** (wor ZHi-dow)	I know.
我知道你要炒面。 **Wǒ zhīdào nǐ yào chǎo miàn.** (wor ZHi-dow nee yow CHow mee-en)	I know you want fried noodles.
我不知道。 **Wǒ bù zhīdào.** (wor *boo* ZHi-dow)	I don't know.
也许 **yěxǔ** (ye-shü)	maybe
我不知道。也许。 **Wǒ bù zhīdào. Yěxǔ.** (wor *boo* ZHi-dow. ye-shü)	I don't know. Maybe.

一点 **yīdiǎn** (ee-dee-en)	a little / a bit of
咖啡 **kāfēi** (kah-fay)	coffee
她要 **Tā yào** (tah yow)	She wants
她要一点咖啡。 **Tā yào yīdiǎn kāfēi.** (tah yow ee-dee-en kah-fay)	She wants a little coffee.
她要一点咖啡吗？ **Tā yào yīdiǎn kāfēi ma?** (tah yow ee-dee-en kah-fay mah)	Does she want a little coffee?
他要 **Tā yào** (tah yow)	He wants
茶 **chá** (CHah)	tea
他要一点茶。 **Tā yào yīdiǎn chá.** (tah yow ee-dee-en CHah)	He wants a little tea.
他要一点茶吗？ **Tā yào yīdiǎn chá ma?** (tah yow ee-dee-en CHah mah)	Does he want a little tea?
他要一点炒饭吗？ **Tā yào yīdiǎn chǎo fàn ma?** (tah yow ee-dee-en CHow fan mah)	Does he want a bit of fried rice?
多一点 **duō yīdiǎn** (dwor ee-dee-en)	a bit more / a little more

他要多一点炒饭吗？ **Tā yào duō yīdiǎn chǎo fàn ma?** (tah yow dwor ee-dee-en CHow fan mah)	Does he want a bit more fried rice?
可乐 **kělè** (ker-ler)	cola / coke
他要多一点可乐吗？ **Tā yào duō yīdiǎn kělè ma?** (tah yow dwor ee-dee-en ker-ler mah)	Does he want a little more coke?
点心 **diǎnxīn** (dee-en-syin)	snack
她要点心。 **Tā yào diǎnxīn.** (tah yow dee-en-syin)	She wants a snack.
广式 **guǎng shì** (gwung SHi)	Cantonese-style
广式点心 **guǎng shì diǎnxīn** (gwung SHi dee-en-syin)	dim sum / Cantonese-style snack
她要广式点心。 **Tā yào guǎng shì diǎnxīn.** (tah yow gwung SHi dee-en-syin)	She wants dim sum.
点 **diǎn** (dee-en)	dot / point / order
我点 **Wǒ diǎn** (wor dee-en)	I order
我点了 **Wǒ diǎn le** (wor dee-en luh)	I ordered

我点了茶、咖啡和广式点心。 **Wǒ diǎn le chá, kāfēi hé guǎng shì diǎnxīn.** (wor dee-en luh CHah, kah-fay her gwung SHi dee-en-syin)	I ordered tea, coffee, and dim sum.
钱 **qián** (chee-en)	money
付钱 **fù qián** (foo chee-en)	pay (literally "pay money")
你付钱 **Nǐ fù qián** (nee foo chee-en)	You pay
你付了钱 **Nǐ fù le qián** (nee foo luh chee-en)	You paid
你付了钱吗? **Nǐ fù le qián ma?** (nee foo luh chee-en mah)	Did you pay?
没 **méi** (may)	didn't
他没付钱 **Tā méi fù qián** (tah may foo chee-en)	He didn't pay
但是 **dànshì** (dan-SHi)	but
他点了茶、咖啡和广式点心,但是他没付钱! **Tā diǎn le chá, kāfēi hé guǎng shì diǎnxīn, dànshì tā méi fù qián!** (tah dee-en luh CHah, kah-fay her gwung SHi dee-en-syin dan-SHi tah may foo chee-en)	He ordered tea, coffee, and dim sum but he didn't pay!

他们 **tāmen** (tah-men)	they
披萨 **pīsà** (pee-sa)	pizza
他们点了披萨，但是他们没付钱！ **Tāmen diǎn le pīsà, dànshì tāmen méi fù qián!** (tah-men *dee-en* luh *pee-sa* dan-SHi tah-men may foo *chee-en*)	They ordered pizza but they didn't pay!
吃 **chī** (CH)	eat
他们吃 **Tāmen chī** (tah-men CH)	They eat
他们吃了 **Tāmen chī le** (tah-men CH luh)	They ate
咕噜肉 **gūlū ròu** (goo-loo-roe)	sweet and sour pork
他们吃了咕噜肉。 **Tāmen chī le gūlū ròu.** (tah-men CH luh *goo-loo-roe*)	They ate sweet and sour pork.
我们 **wǒmen** (wor-men)	we
我们没吃咕噜肉。我们吃了披萨。 **Wǒmen méi chī gūlū ròu. Wǒmen chī le pīsà.** (wor-men may CH *goo-loo-roe*. Wor-men CH luh *pee-sa*)	We didn't eat sweet and sour pork. We ate pizza!

买 **mǎi** (my)	buy
我们买了咖啡。 **Wǒmen mǎi le kāfēi.** (wor-men my luh kah-fay)	We bought coffee.
我们买了咖啡。他们买了披萨。 **Wǒmen mǎi le kāfēi. Tāmen mǎi le pīsà.** (wor-men my luh kah-fay. Tah-men my luh pee-sa)	We bought coffee. They bought pizza.
去 **qù** (chü)	go / go to / to go to
我们去 **Wǒmen qù** (wor-men chü)	We go / We go to
我们去了 **Wǒmen qù le** (wor-men chü luh)	We went / We went to
上海 **Shànghǎi** (SHanghai)	Shanghai
北京 **Běijīng** (bay-jing)	Beijing
我们去了上海，但是他们去了北京。 **Wǒmen qù le Shànghǎi, dànshì tāmen qù le Běijīng.** (wor-men chü luh SHanghai dan-SHi tah-men chü luh bay-jing)	We went to Shanghai but they went to Beijing.
打 **dǎ** (dah)	hit

麻将 **májiàng** (mah-jang)	mahjong
她打麻将。 **Tā dǎ májiàng.** (tah dah mah-jang)	She plays mahjong – literally "She hits mahjong".
她打了麻将。 **Tā dǎ le májiàng.** (tah dah luh mah-jang)	She played mahjong.
她打了麻将吗？ **Tā dǎ le májiàng ma?** (tah dah luh mah-jang mah)	Did she play mahjong?
我的 **wǒde** (wor-duh)	my
我的钱 **wǒde qián** (wor-duh chee-en)	my money
哪里？ **Nǎlǐ?** (nah-lee)	Where?
我的钱去了哪里？ **Wǒde qián qù le nǎlǐ?** (wor-duh chee-en chü luh nah-lee)	Where did my money go?
你的 **nǐde** (nee-duh)	your
你的钱去了哪里？ **Nǐde qián qù le nǎlǐ?** (nee-duh chee-en chü luh nah-lee)	Where did your money go?
我们去了上海，打了麻将。 **Wǒmen qù le Shànghǎi, dǎ le májiàng.** (wor-men chü luh SHanghai, dah luh mah-jang)	We went to Shanghai and played mahjong.

学了 **xué le** (shüwair luh)	learned / studied
功夫 **gōng fū** (gong foo)	kung fu
我们学了功夫。 **Wǒmen xué le gōng fū.** (wor-men shüwair luh gong foo)	We learned kung fu.
太极 **tàijí** (ty-jee)	tai chi
我们学了功夫，但是他们学了太极。 **Wǒmen xué le gōng fū, dànshì tāmen xué le tàijí.** (wor-men shüwair luh gong foo dan-SHi tah-men shüwair luh ty-jee)	We learned kung fu but they learned tai chi.
你们 **nǐmen** (nee-men)	you (MTOP)
你们学了太极吗？ **Nǐmen xué le tàijí ma?** (nee-men shüwair luh ty-jee mah)	Did you learn tai chi? (MTOP)
中文 **Zhōngwén** (ZHong-wen)	Chinese
你们学了中文吗？ **Nǐmen xué le Zhōngwén ma?** (nee-men shüwair luh ZHong-wen mah)	Did you learn Chinese? (MTOP)
英文 **Yīngwén** (ying-wen)	English
你们学了英文吗？ **Nǐmen xué le Yīngwén ma?** (nee-men shüwair luh ying-wen mah)	Did you learn English? (MTOP)

中 **zhōng** (ZHong)	Middle
国 **guó** (gwor)	Country / Kingdom
中国 **Zhōngguó** (ZHong-gwor)	China / Middle Country / Middle Kingdom
他们去了中国。 **Tāmen qù le Zhōngguó.** (tah-men chü luh ZHong-gwor)	They went to China.
他们去了中国吗？ **Tāmen qù le Zhōngguó ma?** (tah-men chü luh ZHong-gwor mah)	Did they go to China?
我打算… **Wǒ dǎsuàn…** (wor dah-swann)	I'm planning to…
我打算去中国。 **Wǒ dǎsuàn qù Zhōngguó.** (wor dah-swann chü ZHong-gwor)	I'm planning to go to China.
五 **wǔ** (woo)	five
月 **yuè** (yü-air)	month
五月 **wǔ yuè** (woo yü-air)	May
我打算五月去中国。 **Wǒ dǎsuàn wǔ yuè qù Zhōngguó.** (wor dah-swann woo yü-air chü ZHong-gwor)	I'm planning to go to China in May.

喔 **Ō** (oh)	*Oh!*
喔，中国哪里？ **Ō, Zhōngguó nǎlǐ?** (oh ZHong-gwor nah-lee)	*Oh, whereabouts in China?*
还 **hái** (hy)	*yet*
我还不知道。 **Wǒ hái bù zhīdào.** (wor hy boo ZHi-dow)	*I don't know yet.*
长城 **Chángchéng** (CHang-CHerng)	*The Great Wall*
我还不知道，也许上海、 北京、长城。 **Wǒ hái bù zhīdào, yěxǔ Shànghǎi, Běijīng, Chángchéng.** (wor hy boo ZHi-dow ye-shü SHanghai bay-jing CHang-CHerng)	*I don't know yet. Maybe Shanghai, Beijing, The Great Wall.*
中国城 **Zhōngguóchéng** (ZHong-gwor-cherng)	*Chinatown*
去过 **qù guò** (chü gwor)	*gone before / been before*
你去过中国城吗？ **Nǐ qù guò Zhōngguóchéng ma?** (nee chü gwor ZHong-gwor-cherng mah)	*Have you been to Chinatown before?*
吃过 **chī guò** (CH gwor)	*eaten before*
你吃过咕噜肉吗？ **Nǐ chī guò gūlū ròu ma?** (nee CH gwor goo-loo roe mah)	*Have you eaten sweet and sour pork before?*

一 **yī** (ee)	one
一月 **yī yuè** (ee yü-air)	January
新加坡 **Xīnjiāpō** (syin-jah-pwor)	Singapore
我打算一月去新加坡。 **Wǒ dǎsuàn yī yuè qù Xīnjiāpō.** (wor dah-swann ee yü-air chü syin-jah-pwor)	I'm planning to go to Singapore in January.
嗯 **Ń** (ng)	Erm
那 **nà** (nah)	that
算 **suàn** (swann)	count
嗯，那不算！ **Ń, nà bù suàn!** (ng nah boo swann)	Erm, that doesn't count.
需要 **xūyào** (shü-yow)	need
明天 **míngtiān** (ming-tee-en)	tomorrow
早上 **zǎoshang** (zow-SHang)	morning

台湾 **Táiwān** (taiwan)	Taiwan
他们需要明天早上去台湾。 **Tāmen xūyào míngtiān zǎoshang qù Táiwān.** (tah-men shü-yow ming-tee-en zow-SHang chü taiwan)	They need to go to Taiwan tomorrow morning.
今天 **jīntiān** (jin-tee-en)	today
晚上 **wǎnshang** (wun-SHang)	evening
今天晚上 **jīntiān wǎnshang** (jin-tee-en wun-SHang)	this evening
我们需要今天晚上去中国城。 **Wǒmen xūyào jīntiān wǎnshang qù Zhōngguóchéng.** (wor-men shü-yow jin-tee-en wun-SHang chü ZHong-gwor-cherng)	We need to go to Chinatown this evening.
时间 **shíjiān** (SHi-jee-en)	time
我需要多一点时间。 **Wǒ xūyào duō yīdiǎn shíjiān.** (wor shü-yow dwor ee-dee-en SHi-jee-en)	I need a little more time.
为什么? **Wèishénme?** (way-SHen-muh)	Why?
晚饭 **wǎnfàn** (wun-fan)	dinner

我还没吃晚饭。 **Wǒ hái méi chī wǎnfàn.** (wor hy may CH wun-fan)	I didn't eat dinner yet.
因为 **yīnwèi** (yin-way)	because
因为我还没吃晚饭。 **Yīnwèi wǒ hái méi chī wǎnfàn.** (yin-way wor hy may CH wun-fan)	because I didn't eat dinner yet.
喔，为什么还没？ **Ō, wèishénme hái méi?** (oh way-SHen-muh hy may)	Oh, why not?
妈妈 **māma** (mah-mah)	mum / mom
来 **lái** (ly)	come / come over
因为我的妈妈来了。 **Yīnwèi wǒde māma lái le.** (yin-way wor-duh mah-mah ly luh)	because my mum came. / because my mum came over.
你知道吗？ **Nǐ zhīdào ma?** (ni ZHi-dow mah)	You know what?
赢 **yíng** (ing)	win
她赢了。 **Tā yíng le.** (tah ing luh)	She won.
所有 **suǒyǒu** (swore-yoe)	all
我所有的钱 **wǒ suǒyǒu de qián** (wor swore-yoe duh chee-en)	all my money

因为我的妈妈来了。我们打了麻将。你知道吗？她赢了我所有的钱。

Yīnwèi wǒde māma lái le. Wǒmen dǎ le májiàng. Nǐ zhīdào ma? Tā yíng le wǒ suǒyǒu de qián!

(yin-way wor-duh mah-mah ly luh. wor-men dah luh mah-jang. Ni ZHi-dow mah. Tah ing luh wor swore-yoe duh chee-en)

Because my mum came over. We played mahjong. You know what? She won all my money!

Having worked your way through the Chinese-to-English list above without making any mistakes, you will now want to get to the point where you can also work through the English-to-Chinese list below without making any mistakes. You should feel free to do this over multiple days or even weeks if you feel you need to. Just take your time and work at it until constructing the sentences and recalling the words become second nature to you.

you	你 **nǐ** (nee)
want	要 **yào** (yow)
You want	你要 **Nǐ yào** (nee yow)
fried	炒 **chǎo** (CHow)
noodles	面 **miàn** (mee-en)
fried noodles / chow mein	炒面 **chǎo miàn** (CHow mee-en)

You want fried noodles / chow mein.	你要炒面。 **Nǐ yào chǎo miàn.** (nee yow CHow mee-en)
tofu	豆腐 **dòufu** (doe-foo)
You want tofu.	你要豆腐。 **Nǐ yào dòufu.** (nee yow doe-foo)
spoken question mark	吗？ **ma?** (mah)
Do you want tofu?	你要豆腐吗？ **Nǐ yào dòufu ma?** (nee yow doe-foo mah)
and	和 **hé** (her)
Do you want fried noodles and tofu?	你要炒面和豆腐吗？ **Nǐ yào chǎo miàn hé dòufu ma?** (nee yow CHow mee-en her doe-foo mah)
rice	饭 **fàn** (fan)
fried rice	炒饭 **chǎo fàn** (CHow fan)
Do you want fried rice and tofu?	你要炒饭和豆腐吗？ **Nǐ yào chǎo fàn hé dòufu ma?** (nee yow CHow fan her doe-foo mah)
not	不 **bù** (boo)

Don't you want fried rice and tofu?	你不要炒饭和豆腐吗？ **Nǐ bù yào chǎo fàn hé dòufu ma?** (nee boo yow CHow fan her doe-foo mah)
I	我 **wǒ** (wor)
I want	我要 **Wǒ yào** (wor yow)
I want fried rice and tofu.	我要炒饭和豆腐。 **Wǒ yào chǎo fàn hé dòufu.** (wor yow CHow fan her doe-foo)
I don't want	我不要 **Wǒ bù yào** (wor boo yow)
I don't want fried rice and tofu.	我不要炒饭和豆腐。 **Wǒ bù yào chǎo fàn hé dòufu.** (wor boo yow CHow fan her doe-foo)
I know.	我知道。 **Wǒ zhīdào.** (wor ZHi-dow)
I know you want fried noodles.	我知道你要炒面。 **Wǒ zhīdào nǐ yào chǎo miàn.** (wor ZHi-dow nee yow CHow mee-en)
I don't know.	我不知道。 **Wǒ bù zhīdào.** (wor boo ZHi-dow)
maybe	也许 **yěxǔ** (ye-shü)
I don't know. Maybe.	我不知道。 也许。 **Wǒ bù zhīdào. Yěxǔ.** (wor boo ZHi-dow. ye-shü)

a little / a bit of	一点 **yīdiǎn** (ee-dee-en)
coffee	咖啡 **kāfēi** (kah-fay)
She wants	她要 **Tā yào** (tah yow)
She wants a little coffee.	她要一点咖啡。 **Tā yào yīdiǎn kāfēi.** (tah yow ee-dee-en kah-fay)
Does she want a little coffee?	她要一点咖啡吗？ **Tā yào yīdiǎn kāfēi ma?** (tah yow ee-dee-en kah-fay mah)
He wants	他要 **Tā yào** (tah yow)
tea	茶 **chá** (CHah)
He wants a little tea.	他要一点茶。 **Tā yào yīdiǎn chá.** (tah yow ee-dee-en CHah)
Does he want a little tea?	他要一点茶吗？ **Tā yào yīdiǎn chá ma?** (tah yow ee-dee-en CHah mah)
Does he want a bit of fried rice?	他要一点炒饭吗？ **Tā yào yīdiǎn chǎo fàn ma?** (tah yow ee-dee-en CHow fan mah)
a bit more / a little more	多一点 **duō yīdiǎn** (dwor ee-dee-en)
Does he want a bit more fried rice?	他要多一点炒饭吗？ **Tā yào duō yīdiǎn chǎo fàn ma?** (tah yow dwor ee-dee-en CHow fan mah)

cola / coke	可乐 **kělè** (ker-ler)
Does he want a little more coke?	他要多一点可乐吗？ **Tā yào duō yīdiǎn kělè ma?** (tah yow dwor ee-dee-en ker-ler mah)
snack	点心 **diǎnxīn** (dee-en-syin)
She wants a snack.	她要点心。 **Tā yào diǎnxīn.** (tah yow dee-en-syin)
Cantonese-style	广式 **guǎng shì** (gwung SHi)
dim sum / Cantonese-style snack	广式点心 **guǎng shì diǎnxīn** (gwung SHi dee-en-syin)
She wants dim sum.	她要广式点心。 **Tā yào guǎng shì diǎnxīn.** (tah yow gwung SHi dee-en-syin)
dot / point / order	点 **diǎn** (dee-en)
I order	我点 **Wǒ diǎn** (wor dee-en)
I ordered	我点了 **Wǒ diǎn le** (wor dee-en luh)
I ordered tea, coffee, and dim sum.	我点了茶、咖啡和广式点心。 **Wǒ diǎn le chá, kāfēi hé guǎng shì diǎnxīn.** (wor dee-en luh CHah, kah-fay her gwung SHi dee-en-syin)

money	钱 **qián** (chee-en)
pay (literally "pay money")	付钱 **fù qián** (foo chee-en)
You pay	你付钱 **Nǐ fù qián** (nee foo chee-en)
You paid	你付了钱 **Nǐ fù le qián** (nee foo luh chee-en)
Did you pay?	你付了钱吗？ **Nǐ fù le qián ma?** (nee foo luh chee-en mah)
didn't	没 **méi** (may)
He didn't pay	他没付钱 **Tā méi fù qián** (tah may foo chee-en)
but	但是 **dànshì** (dan-SHi)
He ordered tea, coffee, and dim sum but he didn't pay!	他点了茶、咖啡和广式点心，但是他没付钱！ **Tā diǎn le chá, kāfēi hé guǎng shì diǎnxīn, dànshì tā méi fù qián!** (tah dee-en luh CHah, kah-fay her gwung SHi dee-en-syin dan-SHi tah may foo chee-en)
they	他们 **tāmen** (tah-men)

pizza	披萨 **pīsà** (pee-sa)
They ordered pizza but they didn't pay!	他们点了披萨，但是他们没付钱！ **Tāmen diǎn le pīsà, dànshì tāmen méi fù qián!** (tah-men dee-en luh pee-sa dan-SHi tah-men may foo chee-en)
eat	吃 **chī** (CH)
They eat	他们吃 **Tāmen chī** (tah-men CH)
They ate	他们吃了 **Tāmen chī le** (tah-men CH luh)
sweet and sour pork	咕噜肉 **gūlū ròu** (goo-loo-roe)
They ate sweet and sour pork.	他们吃了咕噜肉。 **Tāmen chī le gūlū ròu.** (tah-men CH luh goo-loo-roe)
we	我们 **wǒmen** (wor-men)
We didn't eat sweet and sour pork. We ate pizza!	我们没吃咕噜肉。我们吃了披萨。 **Wǒmen méi chī gūlū ròu. Wǒmen chī le pīsà.** (wor-men may CH goo-loo-roe. Wor-men CH luh pee-sa)
buy	买 **mǎi** (my)

We bought coffee.	我们买了咖啡。 **Wǒmen mǎi le kāfēi.** (wor-men my luh kah-fay)
We bought coffee. They bought pizza.	我们买了咖啡。他们买了披萨。 **Wǒmen mǎi le kāfēi. Tāmen mǎi le pīsà.** (wor-men my luh kah-fay. Tah-men my luh pee-sa)
go / go to / to go to	去 **qù** (chü)
We go / We go to	我们去 **Wǒmen qù** (wor-men chü)
We went / We went to	我们去了 **Wǒmen qù le** (wor-men chü luh)
Shanghai	上海 **Shànghǎi** (SHanghai)
Beijing	北京 **Běijīng** (bay-jing)
We went to Shanghai but they went to Beijing.	我们去了上海，但是他们去了北京。 **Wǒmen qù le Shànghǎi, dànshì tāmen qù le Běijīng.** (wor-men chü luh SHanghai dan-SHi tah-men chü luh bay-jing)
hit	打 **dǎ** (dah)
mahjong	麻将 **májiàng** (mah-jang)

She plays mahjong – literally "She hits mahjong".	她打麻将。 **Tā dǎ májiàng.** (tah dah mah-jang)
She played mahjong.	她打了麻将。 **Tā dǎ le májiàng.** (tah dah luh mah-jang)
Did she play mahjong?	她打了麻将吗？ **Tā dǎ le májiàng ma?** (tah dah luh mah-jang mah)
my	我的 **wǒde** (wor-duh)
my money	我的钱 **wǒde qián** (wor-duh chee-en)
Where?	哪里？ **Nǎlǐ?** (nah-lee)
Where did my money go?	我的钱去了哪里？ **Wǒde qián qù le nǎlǐ?** (wor-duh chee-en chü luh nah-lee)
your	你的 **nǐde** (nee-duh)
Where did your money go?	你的钱去了哪里？ **Nǐde qián qù le nǎlǐ?** (nee-duh chee-en chü luh nah-lee)
We went to Shanghai and played mahjong.	我们去了上海，打了麻将。 **Wǒmen qù le Shànghǎi, dǎ le májiàng.** (wor-men chü luh Shanghai, dah luh mah-jang)
learned / studied	学了 **xué le** (shüwair luh)

kung fu	功夫 **gōng fū** (gong foo)
We learned kung fu.	我们学了功夫。 **Wǒmen xué le gōng fū.** (wor-men shüwair luh gong foo)
tai chi	太极 **tàijí** (ty-jee)
We learned kung fu but they learned tai chi.	我们学了功夫，但是他们学了太极。 **Wǒmen xué le gōng fū, dànshì tāmen xué le tàijí.** (wor-men shüwair luh gong foo dan-SHi tah-men shüwair luh ty-jee)
you (MTOP)	你们 **nǐmen** (nee-men)
Did you learn tai chi? (MTOP)	你们学了太极吗？ **Nǐmen xué le tàijí ma?** (nee-men shüwair luh ty-jee mah)
Chinese	中文 **Zhōngwén** (ZHong-wen)
Did you learn Chinese? (MTOP)	你们学了中文吗？ **Nǐmen xué le Zhōngwén ma?** (nee-men shüwair luh ZHong-wen mah)
English	英文 **Yīngwén** (ying-wen)
Did you learn English? (MTOP)	你们学了英文吗？ **Nǐmen xué le Yīngwén ma?** (nee-men shüwair luh ying-wen mah)
Middle	中 **zhōng** (ZHong)

Country / Kingdom	国 **guó** (gwor)
China / Middle Country / Middle Kingdom	中国 **Zhōngguó** (ZHong-gwor)
They went to China.	他们去了中国。 **Tāmen qù le Zhōngguó.** (tah-men chü luh ZHong-gwor)
Did they go to China?	他们去了中国吗？ **Tāmen qù le Zhōngguó ma?** (tah-men chü luh ZHong-gwor mah)
I'm planning to…	我打算… **Wǒ dǎsuàn…** (wor dah-swann)
I'm planning to go to China.	我打算去中国。 **Wǒ dǎsuàn qù Zhōngguó.** (wor dah-swann chü ZHong-gwor)
five	五 **wǔ** (woo)
month	月 **yuè** (yü-air)
May	五月 **wǔ yuè** (woo yü-air)
I'm planning to go to China in May.	我打算五月去中国。 **Wǒ dǎsuàn wǔ yuè qù Zhōngguó.** (wor dah-swann woo yü-air chü ZHong-gwor)
Oh!	喔 **Ō** (oh)

Oh, whereabouts in China?	喔，中国哪里？ **Ō, Zhōngguó nǎlǐ?** (oh ZHong-gwor nah-lee)
yet	还 **hái** (hy)
I don't know yet.	我还不知道。 **Wǒ hái bù zhīdào.** (wor hy boo ZHi-dow)
The Great Wall	长城 **Chángchéng** (CHang-CHerng)
I don't know yet. Maybe Shanghai, Beijing, The Great Wall.	我还不知道，也许上海、北京、长城。 **Wǒ hái bù zhīdào, yěxǔ Shànghǎi, Běijīng, Chángchéng.** (wor hy boo ZHi-dow ye-shü SHanghai bay-jing CHang-CHerng)
Chinatown	中国城 **Zhōngguóchéng** (ZHong-gwor-cherng)
gone before / been before	去过 **qù guò** (chü gwor)
Have you been to Chinatown before?	你去过中国城吗？ **Nǐ qù guò Zhōngguóchéng ma?** (nee chü gwor ZHong-gwor-cherng mah)
eaten before	吃过 **chī guò** (CH gwor)
Have you eaten sweet and sour pork before?	你吃过咕噜肉吗？ **Nǐ chī guò gūlū ròu ma?** (nee CH gwor goo-loo-roe mah)
one	一 **yī** (ee)

January	一月 **yī yuè** (*ee* yü-air)
Singapore	新加坡 **Xīnjiāpō** (syin-jah-pwor)
I'm planning to go to Singapore in January.	我打算一月去新加坡。 **Wǒ dǎsuàn yī yuè qù Xīnjiāpō.** (wor dah-swann *ee* yü-air chü syin-jah-pwor)
Erm	嗯 **Ń** (ng)
that	那 **nà** (nah)
count	算 **suàn** (swann)
Erm, that doesn't count.	嗯，那不算！ **Ń, nà bù suàn!** (ng nah boo swann)
need	需要 **xūyào** (shü-yow)
tomorrow	明天 **míngtiān** (ming-tee-en)
morning	早上 **zǎoshang** (zow-SHang)
Taiwan	台湾 **Táiwān** (taiwan)

They need to go to Taiwan tomorrow morning.	他们需要明天早上去台湾。 **Tāmen xūyào míngtiān zǎoshang qù Táiwān.** (tah-men shü-yow ming-tee-en zow-SHang chü taiwan)
today	今天 **jīntiān** (jin-tee-en)
evening	晚上 **wǎnshang** (wun-SHang)
this evening	今天晚上 **jīntiān wǎnshang** (jin-tee-en wun-SHang)
We need to go to Chinatown this evening.	我们需要今天晚上去中国城。 **Wǒmen xūyào jīntiān wǎnshang qù Zhōngguóchéng.** (wor-men shü-yow jin-tee-en wun-SHang chü ZHong-gwor-cherng)
time	时间 **shíjiān** (SHi-jee-en)
I need a little more time.	我需要多一点时间。 **Wǒ xūyào duō yīdiǎn shíjiān.** (wor shü-yow dwor ee-dee-en SHi-jee-en)
Why?	为什么？ **Wèishénme?** (way-SHen-muh)
dinner	晚饭 **wǎnfàn** (wun-fan)
I didn't eat dinner yet.	我还没吃晚饭。 **Wǒ hái méi chī wǎnfàn.** (wor hy may CH wun-fan)

because	因为 **yīnwèi** (yin-way)
because I didn't eat dinner yet.	因为我还没吃晚饭。 **Yīnwèi wǒ hái méi chī wǎnfàn.** (yin-way wo hy may CH wun-fan)
Oh, why not?	喔，为什么还没？ **Ō, wèishénme hái méi?** (oh way-SHen-muh hy may)
mum	妈妈 **māma** (mah-mah)
come / come over	来 **lái** (ly)
because my mum came. / because my mum came over.	因为我的妈妈来了。 **Yīnwèi wǒde māma lái le.** (yin-way wor-duh mah-mah ly luh)
You know what?	你知道吗？ **Nǐ zhīdào ma?** (Ni ZHi-dow mah)
win	赢 **yíng** (ing)
She won.	她赢了。 **Tā yíng le.** (Tah ing luh)
all	所有 **suǒyǒu** (swore-yoe)
all my money	我所有的钱 **wǒ suǒyǒu de qián** (swore-yoe duh chee-en)

Because my mum came over, we played mahjong. You know what? She won all my money!

因为我的妈妈来了。我们打了麻将。你知道吗？她赢了我所有的钱。

Yīnwèi wǒde māma lái le. Wǒmen dǎ le májiàng. Nǐ zhīdào ma? Tā yíng le wǒ suǒyǒu de qián!

(yin-way wor-duh mah-mah ly luh. wor-men dah luh mah-jang. Ni ZHi-dow mah. Tah ing luh wor swore-yoe duh chee-en)

If you've got through this without making any mistakes then you're ready to read the final, but nevertheless essential, pages of the book, which discuss the tones in Chinese and tell you what to do next.

well done for getting this far! well done indeed...

What those tone marks mean...

You'll have noticed that throughout the book the Chinese words (when written in Pinyin) have tone marks over them and you might well have wondered what to do with them.

Well, on your first time through the book, I didn't want you to do much about them at all. Instead, I wanted you to focus on getting the word order correct and developing a more general feel for the pronunciation of the words. This, in itself, is a significant task when you're first encountering what is a fairly exotic language to average English speaker.

Now that you've finished Chapter 5, however, I want to introduce you to the tones, what they are, and how you can learn to use them.

Essentially, the tones are simply an additional aspect of pronunciation on top of expressing the normal vowel and consonant sounds that you'll find in any language.

We actually use tones ourselves in English. Such as when we change our tone from saying "you want some rice" to "you want some rice?" Did you notice how you changed your tone at the end of that second example? How you used a rising intonation at the end of it? Well, that's how tones work in Chinese, except that every syllable – that is, every part – of every word will have a tone in Chinese.

Below, I'll explain what each of the tones in Chinese sounds like and then how you can learn to use them correctly. Take a look:

The Four Tones

1st Tone   **The Doctor's Tone**

The first tone in Chinese is a tone I like to call "The Doctor's Tone". It's a long flat, high tone – the tone you use at the doctor's when the doctor wants to look in your mouth and tells you to "just say 'aaah'".

Do that yourself now, be a doctor, and tell your patient "just say 'aaah'".

That tone you just made when you said "aaah" is the first tone in Chinese. You can practise it by saying any word in that tone. Try saying the Chinese word for "she" – tā – using that same flat, high tone. Did you manage it? If so, well done, as that's the way that word should be pronounced.

2nd Tone ╱ The Person Upstairs' Tone

The second tone in Chinese is a tone I like to call "The Person Upstairs' Tone". It's a rising tone – the tone you use when you're upstairs and someone calls your name. You can't hear them very clearly and so you say "yeah?" It's a rising tone, the same type of tone you use when you raise your voice at the end of a sentence to turn it into a question.

Practise this yourself now, be the person upstairs and imagine that someone has called your name – respond by saying "yeah?".

That tone you just made when you said "yeah?" is the second tone in Chinese. You can practise it by saying any word in that tone. Try saying the Chinese word for "and" – hé – using that same rising, questioning tone. Did you manage it? If so, well done, as that's the way that word should be pronounced.

3rd Tone ╲╱ The Exasperated Teacher's Tone

The third tone in Chinese is a tone I like to call "The Exasperated Teacher's Tone". It's a falling then rising tone.

Try to imagine a teacher, standing at the front of a class, giving a long explanation. Or at least the teacher is trying to give a long explanation. However, one of her students keeps raising their hand to ask questions. This is quite exasperating for the teacher. You can tell this by her response when she's interrupted for the third time. Pausing in her explanation, yet again, and looking over at the student, she says: "Yes?" in an exasperated tone. This is the third tone in Chinese, a falling rising tone.

Try using it yourself now. Be exasperated, at the end of your tether, as though you are being interrupted for the twentieth time, and then say "yes?" You should notice that your voice falls and then rises. That is the third tone in Chinese.

You can practise it by saying any word in that tone. Try saying the Chinese word for "I" – wǒ – using that same falling, rising, exasperated tone. Did you manage it? If so, well done, as that's the way that word should be pronounced.

4th Tone   The Dog Owner's Tone

The fourth tone in Chinese is a tone I like to call "The Dog Owner's Tone". It's a downward, falling tone – the tone a dog owner uses when they tell their dog to "sit!"

Try using it yourself now. Be a dog owner and tell your dog to "sit!" Say it now!

That tone you just made when you told your dog to "sit!" is the fourth tone in Chinese. You can practise it by saying any word in that tone. Try saying the Chinese word for "want" – **yào** – using that same downward, falling tone. Did you manage it? If so, well done, as that's the way that word should be pronounced.

So, they're the four Chinese tones. In order to get better at using them, there are two things you can do. The first is, when you go through this book a second time, you can keep those tones in mind as you say the words and try to apply them as you work your way back through it. As you will already be familiar with the book's contents, adding the tones at this time won't seem anywhere near as hard as it would have been if you'd tried to apply them your first time through.

The second thing you can do to work on your tones is to follow the instructions on the page that follows this one, the page which tells you what you should do next, once you're finished with this book...

What should I do next?

Well, here you are at the end of the final chapter. You have worked hard and yet a different journey now lies ahead of you!

The question you should be asking, of course, is: "What is that journey exactly?", "Where do I go from here?" – essentially, "What should I do next?"

Well...

Well, that will depend to some degree on what you already knew when you began working through this book.

If you *have* found this book useful then I would recommend moving on to the audio course that I have produced entitled "Learn Mandarin Chinese with Paul Noble". It uses the same method as this book except that you listen to it rather than read it. It will further develop your understanding of how to structure Chinese sentences whilst at the same time gently expanding your vocabulary in the language, as well as teaching you plenty of tricks that will allow you to make rapid progress. It will also provide you with a great deal of opportunity to practise and learn the tones in Chinese directly from the native speakers whose voices you'll hear throughout the audio course.

And after that?

After completing the audio course, I then recommend that you find yourself a Chinese language exchange partner. This you will discover is very easy to do. Chinese speakers all around the world want a chance to practise their English, which means that you have something valuable to trade! Personally, I recommend chatting regularly either in person or online for twenty minutes in English followed by twenty minutes in Chinese.

Try to set a topic that you're going to discuss so that you can look up any relevant vocabulary in advance. Keep those words handy and then try to use them in conversation. If any of them are poorly translated or badly pronounced by you, you will quickly find out.

Make an effort to meet with the same speaker regularly and to return to old topics every couple of months. This will allow you to go back over old vocabulary and will also show you that you are in fact making progress, which will help keep you motivated.

If you follow this piece of advice, as well as the one above it, both you and your Chinese should soar!

Good Luck!